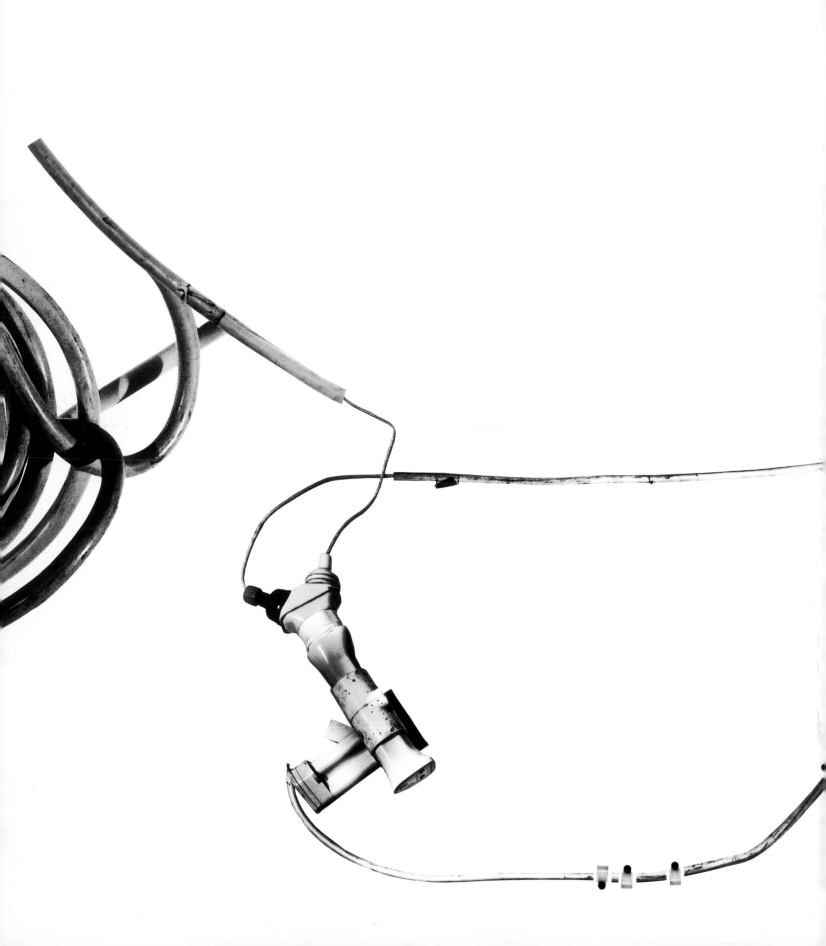

Eurobest/3 The Annual European Advertising & Design Awards

Eurobest/3
I Trofei Annuali della Pubblicità
e del Desegnio Europei
Eurobest/3
Les Trophées Annuels de la
Publicité et du Design Européens
Eurobest/3
Die Jährlichen Preise der
Europäischen Werbung und Design
Eurobest/3
Los Trofeos Anuales de la
Publicidad y del Diseño Europeos

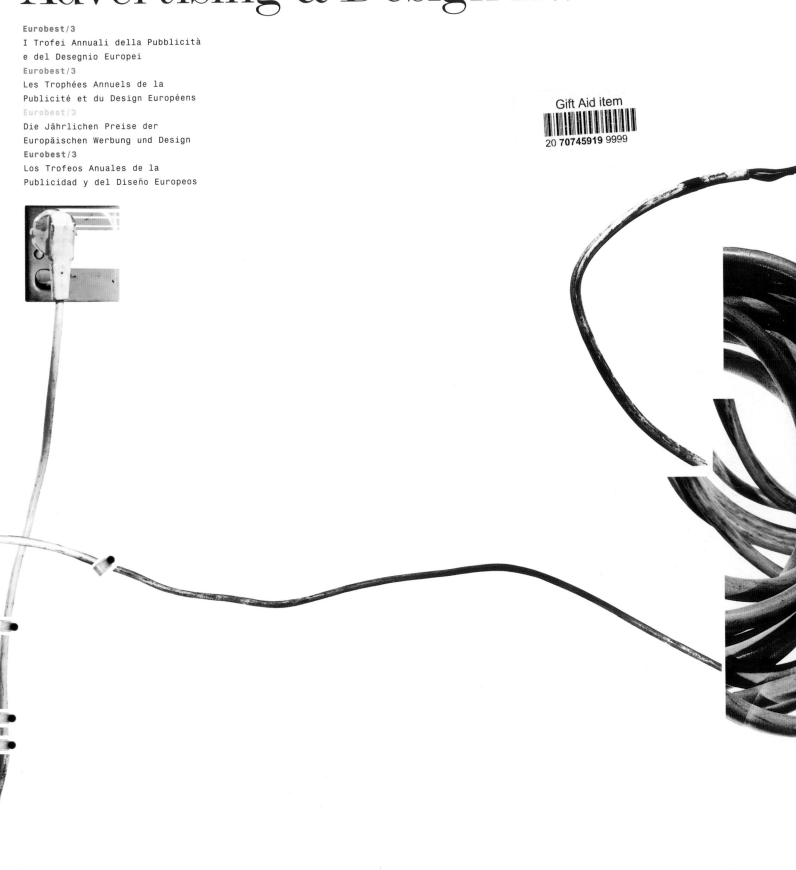

Contents

>
>
>
>
>
>
>
>
>
>
>
>

Book Design by Paul Neale and
Andrew Stevens at Graphic Thought
Facility
>Photography by Andrew Penketh
>Digital Illustration by
Rod Wynne-Powell
>Electronic signage supplied by
EDC Technology
>
>Edited by Liz Farrelly
>Text compiled by Eurobest Awards
Limited
>
>Captions and artwork in this
book have been supplied by the
entrants. While every effort has
been made to ensure accuracy,
Eurobest Awards Limited or the
publisher cannot accept respons-
ibility for errors or omissions
under any circumstances.
>
>Produced and Published by
Booth-Clibborn Editions,
12 Percy Street, London W1P 9FB,
United Kingdom
>Distributed in the United
Kingdom and World-wide Direct
Mail by Internos Books, 12 Percy
Street, London W1P 9FB, UK
>Distributed in France by
InterArt Paris, 1 Rue de L'Est
75020 Paris, France
>USA distribution rights reserved
>Distributed in the rest of the
world by Hearst Books
International, 1350 Avenue of the
Americas, New York, NY 10019, USA
>
>ISBN No 1-873968-71-X
>
>Printed and bound in Hong Kong
by Dai Nippon

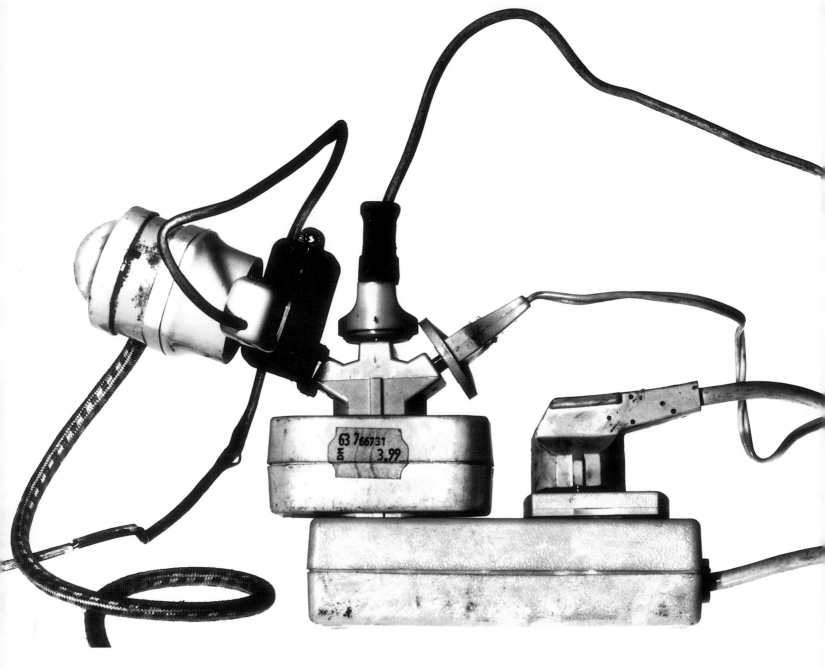

You are simply the best. The advertisements that you are going to see have travelled a long and difficult journey. For this reason alone they receive my most sincere admiration and acknowledgement. I hope they are received in the same way by all the professionals who see them and are considered worthy of their status.

This long journey began in over thirteen European countries. The ads were put together by over 3,000 creatives who pitted their wits against hundreds of product managers, marketing directors, general managers and chairmen. But not all ads are competition winners. An effort must be made to ensure that the 'big idea' has sufficient impact, and offers something new to European advertising and thus deserves to be entered for an award at a festival like Eurobest.

More than 1,500 print ads and 1,500 TV commercials have come down a road that was no less long or rocky than the previous one. More than 100 advertising people from 13 countries worked in marathon sessions to look at and judge the work. 88% of the ads

presented ended their hazardous existence there. Professional colleagues encompassing different cultures, languages and advertising views decided that the ideas were not strong enough or simply missed the idea.

Only 12% of the ads put forward were judged good enough by the 100 advertising professionals to become part of advertising history on the pages of this book.

On the morning of 8 December 1994, two women and 10 men from 12 countries speaking 9 different languages, viewed and judged 153 press ads, 48 outdoor ads and 128 TV commercials.

With eyes glued to screens and hands poised over buttons, only five seconds were allotted for decisions between 0 and 10, love and hate, glory or anonymity, passion or indifference.
>Those of us in European advertising are extremely tough on our own work. Every year we expect more from ourselves. This is, without a doubt, what makes us better. Yet at the same time

it also makes us hypercritical and strict when giving marks and awards for our own work. The best mark for print was 6.73. The best for TV was 8.30.
>The work of the judging panel could easily stop here; all the material on the shortlist had been individually viewed and judged. The highest-scoring ads could have carried off the prizes for each category but

almost all the juries at the biggest festivals in the world add a last hurdle. Another vote is taken by a show of hands for the highest-scoring ads. Only the ads that received eight or more votes obtained a Eurobest. Only 48 Eurobest Awards were given. A lot for a bad year. Few for a year that was so challenging.
>You might think that some ads deserved more and some deserved

less. I personally put my faith in a panel that set out to award prizes only to those who they believed really deserved them.
>With this book you will be able to make up your own minds as to whether we have succeeded or not. But something about which I have no doubt whatsoever is: You are simply the best.
Jordi Vilajoana, BBDO/Espana Chairman of the Jury

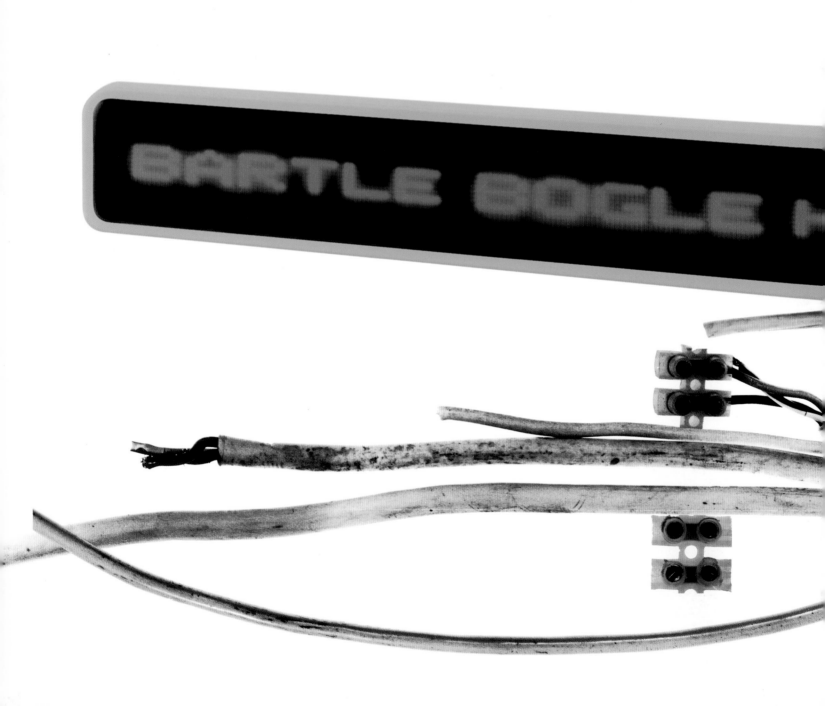

a.

b.

MILK. THE NATURAL HIGH.

a.

b.

c.

Classical choral music.
>We see a middle-class family taking an excursion into the country in their horse-drawn cart, in 1866. Judging by their dress and demeanour, the two daughters have had a very strict and sheltered upbringing.
>We see the family laying out a picnic. After the picnic, the two daughters wander off towards a creek. As they approach the creek, they see a young man in the water.
>The music changes suddenly to a heavy guitar-led rock track.
>We see the older girl's eyes as she stares, spellbound by the young man. We cut to her mouth as her lips slowly part in awe. We pan down the young man's body as water laps over his torso... he appears to be naked. Her sister has found a pair of trousers by the edge of the water. She runs with the trousers, and hides behind a tree with her sister.
>They wait, with a mixture of fear and excitement, as his body comes out of the water. He's wearing 501s. The girls look confused, and glance down at the trousers they are holding.
>They look towards the creek. An old, bearded man is swimming towards them. The trousers clearly belong to him. The girls turn to watch the young man walk towards his horse.
In 1873, Levi's jeans only came shrink-to-fit.
501. The original jean.

Grand Prix Winners
Outdoor/TV and Cinema
p.12/13

c.

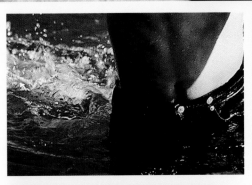

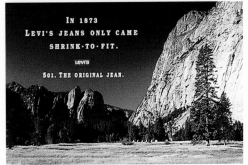

IN 1873
LEVI'S JEANS ONLY CAME
SHRINK-TO-FIT.

LEVI'S

501. THE ORIGINAL JEAN.

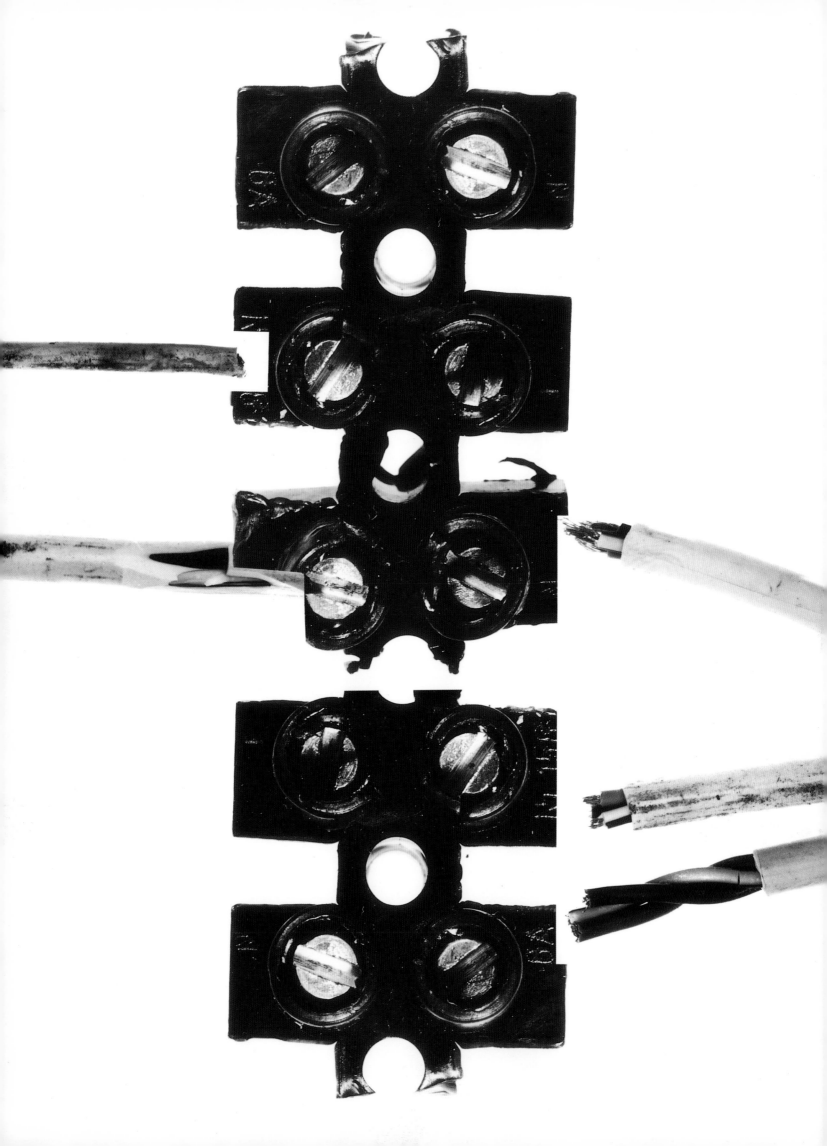

Europe. "An ever closer union."
>At least it is for the majority of the judges assembled in London early in December 1994.
>Like much else in Europe, it was our differences that provided the interest, while our communality of outlook proved once again that good ideas transcend national barriers.
>It became obvious that some markets are more tolerant of generic advertising that services the category rather than the brand and that others are unduly besotted with technique. Yet it was equally obvious that to stand any chance of a prize, you have to be original and relevant.
>It was also nice to hear the distant knocking on the door that was coming from the former Eastern Bloc nations. No prizes this year, but watch this space.
>I enjoyed my stint on Eurobest. I hope you will find much to stimulate you here. And remember, juries aren't infallible. The purpose of a scheme like this is to help you make up your minds what constitutes a good ad.
John Bacon, Foote Cone & Belding

Lorsque vous mettez
deux pains à un steak,
n'oubliez pas
de finir par une claque.

a.

b.

When putting your burger between
2 pieces of bread (in French: 2
punches) don't forget to finish
off with a slap.

Print
Savoury Food
p.16/17

a.
Burger
Advertising Agency
BCRC, Paris
Client
Segma Liebig Maille/McIlhenny
Creative Director
Pascal Gregoire
Copywriter
Patrice Dumas
Art Director
Pierre-Yves Demarcq
Illustrator
Philippe Petit Roule
Advertiser's Supervisor
Frédéric Ordner

Saatchi & Saatchi Advertising,
Amstelveen
Client
Friesche Vlag
Creative Director
Wim Ubachs
Copywriter
Marcel Jiskoot
Art Director
Margriet Groen
Photographer
Dieter Eikelpoth
Account Supervisor
Piet Hein Smit
Advertiser's Supervisor
Leo van Sister/Luc Putmans

100ml. Balance halfvol bevat: 470kJ, eiwitten 8g, koolhydraten 11g, vetten 4g (1,8g linoleenzuur, 0,9g linolzuur) Beperk je cholesterol

c.

Nu börjar älgjakten.

Sveriges mest älskade ko.

a.
It's open season on elk.
>This ad was published at the
start of the elk hunting season.
Some farmers actually take the
precaution of marking their cows
to prevent elk hunters from
shooting cattle by mistake!

a.
Elk
Advertising Agency
Forsman & Bodenfors, Gothenberg
Client
Arla
Copywriter
Björn Engström/Filip Nilsson
Art Director
Staffan Forsman
Photographer
Håkan Ludwigsson/Tomas Yeh
Account Supervisor
Olle Victorin
Advertiser's Supervisor
Anne-Marie Lindstedt

Print
Savoury Food
p.18/19

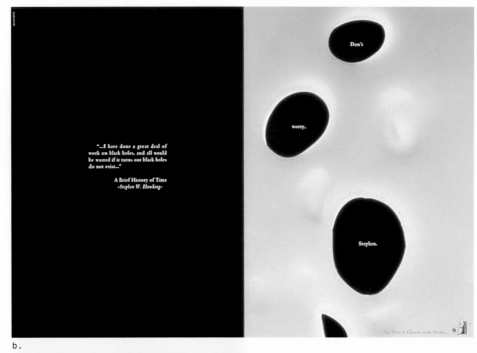

"...I have done a great deal of work on black holes, and all would be wasted if it turns out black holes do not exist..."

A Brief History of Time
-Stephen W. Hawking-

b.

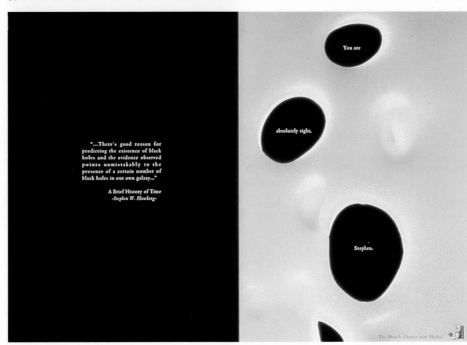

"...One night in November, 1970, I began to think about black holes while I was in bed..."

A Brief History of Time
-Stephen W. Hawking-

c.

"...There's good reason for predicting the existence of black holes and the evidence observed points unmistakably to the presence of a certain number of black holes in our own galaxy..."

A Brief History of Time
-Stephen W. Hawking-

d.

YOU'RE LISTENING TO A SMOKE ALARM THAT WASN'T FITTED WITH A DURACELL BATTERY.

The silence is deafening.

Sadly, they used an ordinary SP battery instead of a Duracell, which lasts up to six times longer.

This week happens to be National Fire Safety Week so there's all the more reason to check that your smoke alarm runs on Duracell – the only battery displaying the B? Kitemark for quality.

After all, you wouldn't want a battery's life expectancy to affect yours, now would you?

DURACELL NO ORDINARY BATTERY LOOKS LIKE IT OR LASTS LIKE

a.

Ils se cachèrent dans un bois et eurent plein de Yoplait avec des fruits des bois.

b.
They hid in the woods and had lots of Yoplait with forest fruits.

Print
Savoury Food/
Sweet Food and Confectionery/
Household, Maintenance Products
and Pet Products
p.20/21

a.
Smoke Alarm
Advertising Agency
Bates Dorland, London
Client
Duracell
Creative Director
Loz Simpson/Gerard Stamp
Copywriter
Paul Alderman
Art Director
Peter Ogden
Photographer
Stuart Redler
Account Supervisor
Julian Sandy
Advertiser's Supervisor
Gary Ferguson

b.
Les Fruits De La Forêt
Advertising Agency
**Jean & Montmarin,
Levallois-Perret**
Client
Yoplait
Creative Director
Gérard Jean
Copywriter
Anne Boutervasser
Art Director
Gérard Jean
Photographer
Gérard Jean
Account Supervisor
Pierre Woreczek
Advertiser's Supervisor
Pierre Yves Ballif

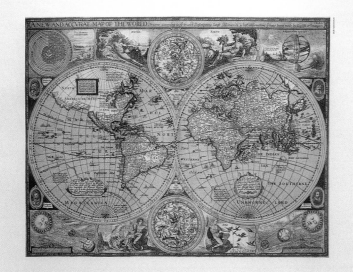

Si Dieu a mis autant d'eau salée sur la Terre il doit bien y avoir une raison.

c.
There must be a good reason for
God putting so much salty water
on the earth.

c.
There Must Be A Good Reason...
Advertising Agency
DDB Needham France, Paris
Client
Barilla
Creative Director
Christian Vince
Copywriter
Jean Denis Pallain
Art Director
Olivier Verdon
Account Supervisor
Charles de Monsabert
Advertiser's Supervisor
Benjamin Pardo/Aude Rion

a.

Print
Sweet Food and Confectionery/
Alcohol: Spirits/
Alcohol: Beers and Wine
p.22/23

As we may not be permitted to advertise after November 28, we're showing you the Derby Club ads of the next 50 years today already.

b.
(On November 28, 1993, Swiss
voters had to decide whether or
not tobacco and alcohol
advertising would be banned.)

De tips voor vaderdag.

Voetenbankje.

CD-rek.

Gereedschapskist.

TV-meubel.

Visstoeltje.

Werkbank.

Koelbox.

Bijzettafeltje.

Minibar.

Zo, nu eerst 'n Bavaria

c.
Tips for Father's day.
Footstool, CD-rack, toolbox,
etc.

a.
Mother Nature Father Baker
Advertising Agency
Springer & Jacoby, Hamburg
Client
Wasa
Creative Director
Stefan Zschaler
Copywriter
Bettina Bergmann
Art Director
Claas Janßen/Wiebke Schulz
Photographer
Olaf Tamm
Account Supervisor
Bettina Kasakewitsch
Advertiser's Supervisor
Thomas Ormann

b.
Twin Initiative:
Before
Advertising Agency
Advico Young & Rubicam, Zürich
Client
Pick & Pay
Creative Director
Hansjörg Zürcher
Copywriter
Matthias Freuler
Art Director
Erik Voser
Photographer
Alf Dietrich
Account Supervisor
Uschi Krebs
Advertiser's Supervisor
Reto Cina

c.
Father's Day
Advertising Agency
DMB&B Advertising, Amsterdam
Client
Bavaria Beer
Copywriter
Pascal Boogaert/Klaas Slooten
Art Director
Martijn Rooij/André van Leeuwen
Photographer
Hans Hiltermann
Account Supervisor
Harry Oostendorp
Advertiser's Supervisor
P.P.J.M. Swinkels

ABSOLUT PARIS.

a.

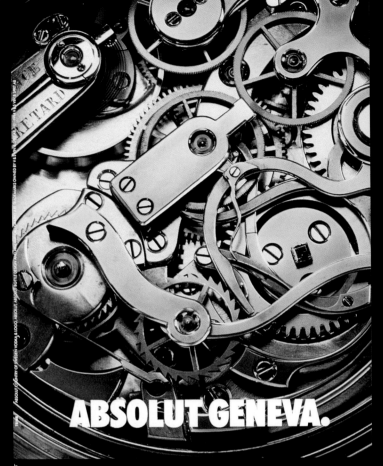

b.

c.

a,b,c.

Eurobest Campaign Award Winner
Absolut Paris
Absolut Brussels
Absolut Geneva
Advertising Agency
TBWA, Paris
Client
Swedish Wine and Spirits
Creative Director
Jacques Henocq
Copywriter
Bruno Richard
Art Director
Pascale Gayraud

ARTIFICIAL CREAM.

Boddingtons. The Cream of Manchester. Brewed at the Strangeways Brewery since 1778.

a.

SINGLE CREAM.

Boddingtons. The Cream of Manchester. Brewed at the Strangeways Brewery since 1778.

a,b,c.

Eurobest Campaign Award Winner
Artificial Cream
Single Cream
Cheese
Advertising Agency
Bartle Bogle Hegarty, London
Client
The Whitbread Beer Company
Creative Director
John Hegarty
Copywriter
Tim Riley
Art Director
Mike Wells

 THE CREAM OF MANCHESTER.

Boddingtons Draught Bitter. Brewed at the Strangeways Brewery since 1778.

a.

b.

e.

f.

Print
Clothing, Footwear and
Accessories
p.28/29

a,b.
Eurobest Campaign Award Winner
Fat People
The Room
Advertising Agency
**Paradiset DDB Needham,
Stockholm**
Client
Diesel
Creative Director
Joakim Jonason
Copywriter
Linus Karlsson
Art Director
Joakim Jonason
Photographer
Pierre Winther
Account Supervisor
Stefan Öström/Jacqueline Nyman
Advertiser's Supervisor
**Johan Lindeberg/
Maurizio Marchiori**

c,d,e,f,g.
Eurobest Campaign Award Winner
Pet Shop
Solarium
Generals
Pool
Car Crash
Advertising Agency
**Paradiset DDB Needham,
Stockholm**
Client
Diesel
Creative Director
Joakim Jonason
Copywriter
Linus Karlsson
Art Director
Joakim Jonason
Photographer
Pierre Winther
Account Supervisor
Stefan Öström/Gunilla Orander
Advertiser's Supervisor
**Johan Lindeberg/
Maurizio Marchiori**

c.

d.

g.

a.

b.

c.

a,b,c.
Pathologist
Equal Opportunist
Dyslexic
Advertising Agency
Saatchi & Saatchi, London
Client
Carlsberg-Tetley Brewing
Creative Director
James Lowther/Simon Dicketts
Copywriter
Richard Dean
Art Director
Martha Riley
Photographer
Malcolm Venville
Account Supervisor
David Goring-Morris
Advertiser's Supervisor
Liz Morgan

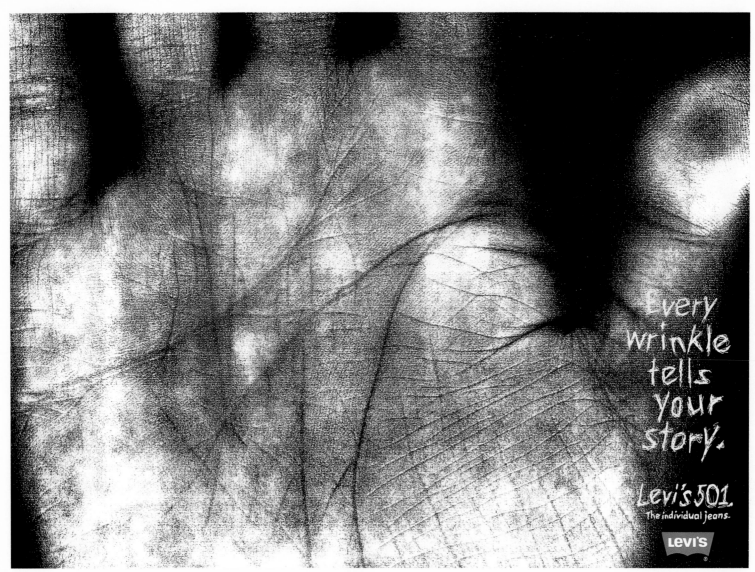

a.

b.

Print
Clothing, Footwear and
Accessories/
Household, Maintenance Products
and Pet Products
p.32/33

c.
Look me in the eyes... I said
the eyes.

d.

a.

Eurobest Award Winner
Hand
Advertising Agency
McCann-Erickson Frankfurt
Client
Levi Strauss Deutschland
Creative Director
Rainer Bollmann
Copywriter
Martina Möhr
Art Director
**Wolf-Peter Camphausen/
Martina Möhr**
Photographer
Clive Davis
Account Supervisor
Oliver Mohr
Advertiser's Supervisor
Ralph Ohnemus

b.

Urinal
Advertising Agency
McCann-Erickson Frankfurt
Client
Levi Strauss Deutschland
Creative Director
Rainer Bollmann
Copywriter
Martina Möhr
Art Director
**Wolf-Peter Camphausen/
Martina Möhr**
Photographer
Clive Davis
Account Supervisor
Oliver Mohr
Advertiser's Supervisor
Ralph Ohnemus

c.

The Eyes
Advertising Agency
TBWA, Paris
Client
Playtex France
Creative Director
Jacques Henocq
Copywriter
Frédéric Beigbeder
Art Director
Delphine Valette
Photographer
Ellen von Unwerth
Account Supervisor
Maryse Sarraut
Advertiser's Supervisor
**G. Fertout/J.L. Prodhomme/
C. Menard**

d.

Fork
Advertising Agency
Delvico Bates Barcelona
Client
Benckiser
Creative Director
**Toni Segarra/
Félix Fernandez
de Castro**
Copywriter
Toni Segarra
Art Director
David Caballero
Photographer
Jané & Osés
Account Supervisor
Ana Moreno

1883: indigo dye used for the first time [and Karl Marx dies].

Levi's The original jeans.

a.

Print
Clothing, Footwear and
Accessories
p.34/35

a.
Marx
Advertising Agency
Bartle Bogle Hegarty, London
Client
Levi Strauss & Co. Europe
Creative Director
John Hegarty
Copywriter
Bruce Crouch
Art Director
Graham Watson
Photographer
Magnum
Account Supervisor
Gwyn Jones
Advertiser's Supervisor
Roy Edmunson

b,c,d.
Super Loose
Regular
Loose
Advertising Agency
Bartle Bogle Hegarty, London
Client
Levi Strauss & Co. Europe
Creative Director
John Hegarty
Copywriter
Roger Beckett
Art Director
Andy Smart
Photographer
Eugene Richards
Account Supervisor
Gwyn Jones
Advertiser's Supervisor
Roy Edmunson

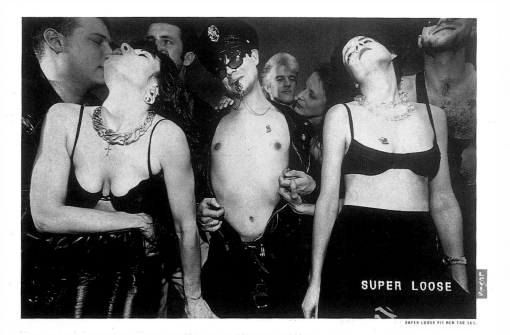

b.

c.

d.

LEVI'S 501 JEANS. THE MORE YOU USE THEM, THE BETTER THEY GET.

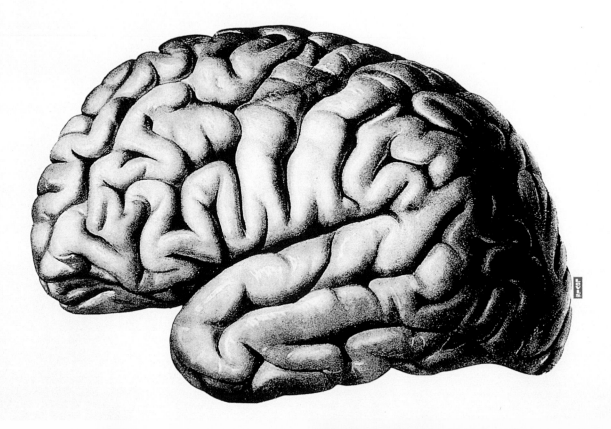

a.

b.

c.

d.
Using Neo Tricosteril bandaids
on all kinds of nuisances will
provide immediate comfort.

a,b.
Brains
Punching Ball
Advertising Agency
Bassat Ogilvy & Mather,
Barcelona
Client
Levi Strauss de España
Creative Director
Gustavo Caldas/David Ruiz
Copywriter
Gustavo Caldas
Art Director
David Ruiz
Photographer
Arara Pelegrin/Carlos Suarez/
Horrillo Riola
Account Supervisor
Bettina Farreras
Advertiser's Supervisor
Anne de Rider

c.
Cactus
Advertising Agency
Delvico Bates Barcelona
Client
Icart
Creative Director
Toni Segarra/
Félix Fernandez de Castro
Copywriter
Toni Segarra
Art Director
David Caballero
Account Supervisor
Ana Moreno

d.
Tricosteril
Advertising Agency
BCRC, Paris
Client
Laboratoires Polive
Creative Director
Pascal Gregoire
Copywriter
Stéphane Xiberras
Art Director
Jean-Loup Seuret
Photographer
Bruno Suet
Account Supervisor
Michèle Dupont Bruin
Advertiser's Supervisor
Denis Boutte

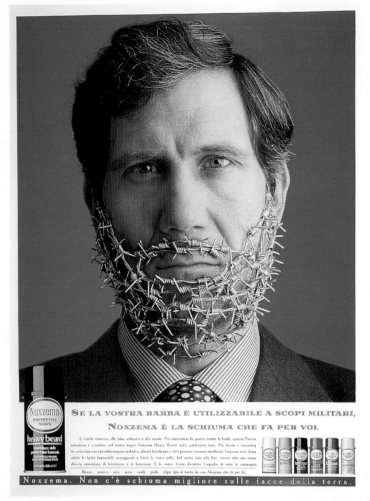

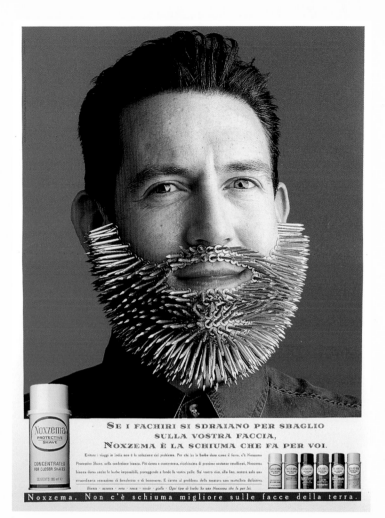

a.
If your beard could be used for
military purposes, Noxzema is
the shaving foam for you.
Noxzema. No better shaving foam
on the faces of the earth.

b.
If a fakir lies on your face by
mistake, Noxzema is the shaving
foam for you. Noxzema. No
better shaving foam on the faces
of the earth.

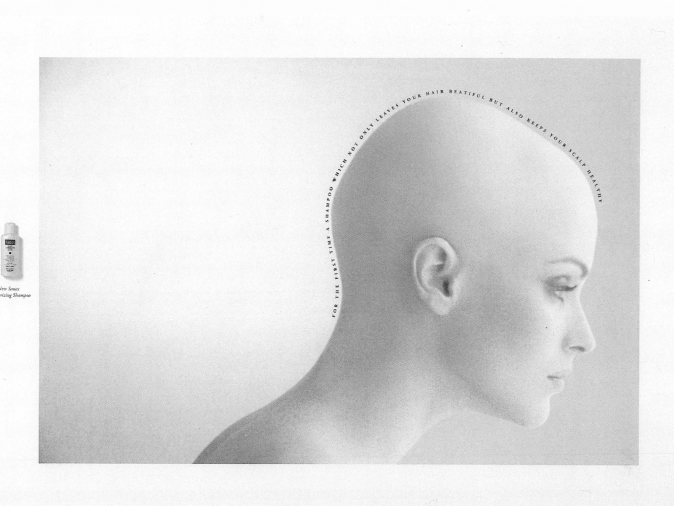

New Sanex
Moisturizing Shampoo

FOR THE FIRST TIME A SHAMPOO WHICH NOT ONLY LEAVES YOUR HAIR BEATIFUL BUT ALSO KEEPS YOUR SCALP HEALTHY

c.

a,b.
Barbed Wire
Nails
Advertising Agency
Universal Advertising, Milan
Client
Schiapparelli Benessere
Creative Director
Jane Tracy
Copywriter
Paolo Chiabrando
Art Director
Elia Coro
Photographer
Graham Ford
Model Maker
Guy Hodgkinson
Account Supervisor
Leone Bringheli
Advertiser's Supervisor
Sandra Gotelli

c.
Bald Head
Advertising Agency
Casadevall Pedreño & PRG,
Barcelona
Client
Cruz Verde/Legrain
Creative Director
Luis Casadevall/Xavi García/
Ramón Roda
Copywriter
Luis Casadevall/Xavi García
Art Director
Ramón Roda
Photographer
Francisco Daniel
Account Supervisor
Salvador Pedreño/
Maria Llisa Voltes
Advertiser's Supervisor
Fernando Vaquer

IF I CAN find my Jeep Cherokee in the morning, I can drive it.

UP HERE IN THE HIGH ROCKIES, it's not unusual for several feet of snow to fall overnight. How do you get around? Get yourself a Jeep Cherokee. And try to remember where you parked it.

WITH AN AVERAGE winter snowfall of 41 feet, Idaho can be a skier's dream, but a motorist's nightmare. The locals have a simple solution. Don't drive an ordinary car. Drive a Jeep Cherokee. THE JEEP'S full-time or part-time four wheel drive system gives unrivalled traction when the going gets rough. Or wet, or icy. AND WHEN you're downhill racing, its always nice to know you can stop, simply by stepping on the ABS brakes. On your way down the mountain, you'll notice that instead of the usual soggy 4x4 handling, the Cherokee feels taut, fast and responsive.

NOT ONLY DOES this make it more surefooted in the snow, it also makes it more exciting after the thaw. And whilst life in the Rockies may be harsh, life in the Cherokee is anything but. WHICH OTHER mountain vehicle cossets you with power adjustable front seats, air conditioning, cruise control and automatic transmission? AND GIVES YOU the security of side impact protection guards and a 3 year warranty? You can search high and low for a better value 4x4, but we don't think you'll find it. ✪ **Jeep** The American Legend.

JEEP CHEROKEE FOUR LITRE LIMITED £19,565.

a.

OUR nearest neighbour is 34 miles by road. Or 7 miles by Jeep Cherokee.

SURE, THE ROADS ROUND here get you from A to B trouble is they tend to go via Z. So the quickest way to go places is to drive a Jeep Cherokee. And take the scenic route.

c.

JEEP Cherokee. We use it for huntin', shoppin' and fishin'.

THE ONLY PROBLEM with living miles from civilisation, is that you're miles from civilisation. The answer? Drive a Cherokee and mix business with your local store.

d.

THE CHRYSLER VIPER:

NO ROOM FOR MORE THAN TWO

NO ROOM FOR ANY LUGGAGE

NO SIDE WINDOWS

NO ROOF

NO EXTERIOR DOORHANDLES

NO MAKE UP MIRROR

NO COLOURS BUT RED

Mijn grootvader had een Passat.

Mijn vader had een Passat.

En nu heb ik hem.

De meeste auto's gaan elf jaar mee.

Wij kennen Passats die op hun sloffen de acht-tien halen.

In al die jaren maakt zo'n Passat natuurlijk heel veel kilometers en meestal heel weinig problemen. Neem bijvoorbeeld de motor. Die bleek zo sterk dat we zelfs onze dieselmotoren, die aan veel grotere krachten blootstaan, ervan afgekeken hebben.

In al die jaren versjouwt zo'n Passat meestal ook hele scheepsladingen. Onvermoeibaar en dankzij z'n postuur vaak in één keer.

En in al die jaren heeft zo'n Passat niet meer onderhoud nodig dan een andere auto in zijn veel kortere leven. Een Volkswagen heeft nu eenmaal genoeg aan één grote beurt per 30.000 kilometer.

Is het raar als je gehecht raakt aan een voertuig

dat zo trouw is?

Het is maar een auto, hoor je vaak zeggen. Het is maar een Passat, horen wij zelden.

Anderen maken misschien een familieauto. Volkswagen maakt een auto die je jaren in de familie kunt houden. De Volkswagen Passat.

Volkswagen. Wie anders?

IMPORTEUR: PON'S AUTOMOBIELHANDEL B.V. POSTBUS 72, 3800 HD AMERSFOORT. TELEFOON: 033 - 94 99 44.

IN SOME PARTS OF THE WORLD, LAND ROVERS ARE THE ONLY VEHICLES PEOPLE HAVE EVER SEEN.

LAND ROVER FIRST MADE A 4x4 VEHICLE IN 1947. SINCE THEN WE'VE MADE NOTHING ELSE.

b.

OF ALL THE LAND ROVERS BUILT OVER THE LAST 30 YEARS, 74% ARE STILL ON THE ROAD.

c.

a.

	b.	c.
Eurobest Award Winner		
River	Track	Hard Cell
Advertising Agency	Advertising Agency	Advertising Agency
Bates Dorland, London	**Bates Dorland, London**	**Bates Dorland, London**
Client	Client	Client
Land Rover	**Land Rover**	**Land Rover**
Creative Director	Creative Director	Creative Director
Loz Simpson/Gerard Stamp	**Loz Simpson/Gerard Stamp**	**Loz Simpson**
Copywriter	Copywriter	Copywriter
Loz Simpson	**Loz Simpson**	**David Prideaux**
Art Director	Art Director	Art Director
Gerard Stamp	**Gerard Stamp**	**Nick Simons**
Photographer	Photographer	Photographer
Max Forsythe	**Max Forsythe**	**Graham Ford**
Account Supervisor	Account Supervisor	Account Supervisor
Philip Lancaster	**Philip Lancaster**	**Philip Lancaster**
Advertiser's Supervisor	Advertiser's Supervisor	Advertiser's Supervisor
Russell Turnham	**Russell Turnham**	**Russell Turnham**

Man sitzt gut.

Man fühlt sich gut.

Und man hat jede Menge Spaß.

Rot Gelb Grün

in einem Mercedes von AMG.

► Alles schien völlig normal: Es sah aus wie ein Mercedes. Es fühlte sich an wie ein Mercedes. Es roch wie ein Mercedes. Und dann war es doch kein Mercedes. Zumindest kein völlig normaler.

Gleich nach den ersten Metern war klar, was sich hinter dem AMG-Logo auf dem Kofferraumdeckel verbarg: hochkarätige, rennsporterprobte Technik. Das ging schon beim 3,6-I-AMG-Saugmotor los. Seine extrem kurzen Leichtmetallkolben drehten bereitwillig

hoch, und 385 Newtonmeter Drehmoment zauberten bereits bei niedrigen Drehzahlen ein Lächeln auf Herrchens Gesicht. Das Fahrwerk war auch straffer als üblich, und die Bremsen – hoppla –, o ja, die waren noch etwas bissiger als gewohnt.

► Und das Schönste: Bei aller Sportlichkeit kam nie das Gefühl auf, in einer brettharten Fahrmaschine zu sitzen. In puncto Komfort, Sicherheit und Zuverlässigkeit ist also auch ein AMG-Mercedes vor allem ein Mercedes.

► Soweit mein erster Eindruck, den ich auf die Schnelle gewinnen konnte. Eine eigene Meinung bilden Sie sich dann am besten während einer Probefahrt mit einem der verschiedenen Modelle. Im nächstgelegenen AMG-Center gibt man dafür gern grünes Licht.

Mercedes-Benz

Ihr guter Stern auf allen Straßen.

a.
Red, amber, green — in Mercedes
by AMG.

Print
Automotive
p.46/47

a.
Traffic Lights
Advertising Agency
Springer & Jacoby, Hamburg
Client
Mercedes-Benz
Creative Director
René Clohse
Copywriter
Michael Bondzio
Art Director
Axel Thomsen
Photographer
Pete Sieward
Account Supervisor
Hans-Christian Schwingen
Advertiser's Supervisor
Jochen Pläcking

b.
Short Model
Advertising Agency
Springer & Jacoby, Hamburg
Client
Mercedes-Benz
Creative Director
**Gabi Junklewitz/
Hans-Jürgen Lewandowski**
Copywriter
Michael Bondzio
Art Director
Bernd Beitz
Photographer
Daniel Hartz
Account Supervisor
Markus Schneider
Advertiser's Supervisor
Jochen Pläcking

c.
Life Begins At 40
Advertising Agency
**Klaus E Küster Werbeagentur,
Frankfurt**
Client
Dr. Ing. h.c.F. Porsche
Creative Director
Klaus Erich Küster
Copywriter
Klaus Erich Küster
Art Director
John Buchner/Carlos Ferreira
Photographer
Jerry Oke
Account Supervisor
Wolfgang Rehborn/Ludger Cosanne
Advertiser's Supervisor
Gerd E. Mäuser/Peter Metzdorf

Die S-Klasse ist manchen zu lang. Aber die Kurzversion überzeugt jeden.

Die S-Klasse im Original.

Die S-Klasse im Ernstfall.

▶ Mal angenommen, Sie stellen ein Automobil, das fünf Personen einigermaßen bequem Platz bietet, neben die S-Klasse oben links. Wahrscheinlich wird es etwas kürzer sein. Nun nehmen Sie dasselbe Fahrzeug nach einem Front- und einem Heckaufprall mit jeweils 50 km/h und stellen es neben die S-Klasse oben rechts. Wahrscheinlich wird es noch immer ein bißchen kürzer sein. Hoffentlich nicht zu kurz.

Ginge im Straßenverkehr immer alles glatt, wäre es ein leichtes, Autos zu bauen, die bei minimaler Länge ein Maximum an Raumkomfort bieten. Das Problem beginnt, wenn dieser Raum bei einem Unfall schlagartig zum Überlebensraum wird, den es um jeden Preis zu erhalten gilt. Denn dann zählt jeder Zentimeter.

▶ Die Größe des Innenraums ist bei einer Reiselimousine wie der S-Klasse natürlich durch ihren Zweck vorgegeben: Sie soll fünf ausgewachsenen Personen den Platz bieten, der nötig ist, um lange Geschäftsreisen entspannt zu absolvieren und nebenher noch effektiv arbeiten zu können. Und gleichzeitig soll auch das Gepäck gut untergebracht sein.

Solch ein Fahrzeug kann zwangsläufig kein Leichtgewicht sein. Entsprechend groß ist die Energiemenge, die im Falle eines Unfalles in Sekundenbruchteilen absorbiert werden muß. Und entsprechend viele Zentimeter Blech müssen planmäßig zerknautscht werden, bis die überschüssige Energie so weit umgewandelt ist, daß sie den Insassen nicht mehr gefährlich werden kann.

▶ Daß wir nach über 30 Jahren systematischer Crashtests ziemlich genau wissen, an welchen Stellen wir nicht sparen dürfen, ist aber nicht der einzige Grund dafür, daß die Knautschzone der S-Klasse etwas größer ausfällt als bei vielen anderen. Es liegt auch daran, daß wir ihre Konstruktion inzwischen so weiterentwickelt haben, daß sie beim Zusammenprall mit kleineren Fahrzeugen auch noch Funktionen übernimmt, die die Knautschzone des Unfallgegners allein nicht leisten kann. Wir nennen das Partnerschutz.

▶ Sollte also unter Umständen während Ihrer Probefahrt beim Mercedes-Benz Partner die S-Klasse für die erstbeste Parklücke etwas zu lang sein, dann denken Sie dran: Die paar Zentimeter mehr könnten möglicherweise für Sie und andere einmal sehr wichtig werden. Aber das sollten Sie besser nicht gleich ausprobieren.

Mercedes-Benz
Ihr guter Stern auf allen Straßen.

b.
Some find the S-class too long.
But everybody is impressed by
the short model.

Rufen Sie uns an, wenn Sie weitere Informationen über das 911 Cabriolet möchten. Porsche Online: 0132 - 356 911

17 Jahre: Der erste Kuß.

19 Jahre: Das erste Auto.

26 Jahre: Der erste Job.

42 Jahre: Der erste Porsche.

Ist es nicht schön, daß das Leben nach oben offen ist?

PORSCHE

c.
17, your first kiss.
19, your first car.
26, your first job.
42, your first Porsche.
See, life does begin at 40.

Citroën souhaite à tous, bonne route et bonnes vacances.

a.

One mark: Danger. Two marks:
Security. Citroen wishes
everyone a safe journey and a
nice holiday.

 c.

a.
The Chevrons
Advertising Agency
**Euro RSCG Scher Lenoir &
Lafarge, Levallois-Perret**
Client
Citroen
Creative Director
Gilbert Scher
Copywriter
Jean-Christophe Royer
Art Director
Christophe Caubel
Illustrator
Christophe Austrui
Account Supervisor
Christophe Lafarge
Advertiser's Supervisor
Andre Cherid/Jean Marc Savigne

b.
Boy On Bicycle
Advertising Agency
Campaign Company, Amsterdam
Client
Mercedes Benz Nederland
Copywriter
Poppe van Pelt
Art Director
Diederick Hillenius
Photographer
Marcel van der Vlugt
Packshot
Paul Ruigrok
Account Supervisor
Dik Klicks
Advertiser's Supervisor
Luc Schram

Eurobest Award Winner
Crossroads
Advertising Agency
Ogilvy & Mather Amsterdam
Client
Ford Netherlands
Creative Director
Krijn van Noordwijk
Copywriter
Willem van Harrewijen
Art Director
Jeroen Peters
Photographer
Boudewijn Smit
Account Supervisor
**Janine Vermeltfoort/
Peter Neuteboom**
Advertiser's Supervisor
Jan Peter Maas/John Hoes

Print
Automotive
p.48/49

b.

Yesterday's feeling of safety.

De Maverick 4×4.

c.

Bob Hahn restaureert alleen klassieke Porsches.
Tel. 036-5346729

a.

b.

Eurobest Award Winner
Carl Lewis
Advertising Agency
Young & Rubicam, London
Client
Pirelli
Creative Director
Mike Cozens
Copywriter
Ewan Paterson
Art Director
Graeme Norways
Photographer
Annie Leibovitz
Account Supervisor
David Gray/Emma Brock
Advertiser's Supervisor
Giancarlo Rocco

a.

Miss Germany: 40 Years Later
Advertising Agency
Orgasms Advertising, Amsterdam
Client
Bob Hahn Classic Porsche
Restoration
Copywriter
Joost Perik/Dieuwke Reehoorn
Art Director
Hjarald Agnes
Photographer
Henri ter Hall
Account Supervisor
Bob Hahn

c.

Pit Stop
Advertising Agency
DDB Needham Worldwide,
Amsterdam
Client
Pon's Automobielhandel
Creative Director
Lode Schaeffer/Erik Wünsch
Copywriter
Sikko Gerkema
Art Director
Matthijs van Wensveen
Photographer
Boudewijn Smit
Account Supervisor
Amos Frank/Bart Boezeman
Advertiser's Supervisor
A.E.G. Vugs/G.S. Smit

b.
Also finalist in the Photography
Category

De pitstop bij Volkswagen: 23 minuten en 17 seconden.

Bij Lotus, McLaren en Ferrari lachen ze erom.

Wij zijn er trots op.

Bij McLaren wordt er tijdens de pitstop namelijk geen autoradio ingebouwd. Of een zonnedak gemonteerd.

En dat is bij onze pitstop (wij noemen het: Express Service) allemaal volstrekt normaal.

Die Express Service vindt u door het hele land. Gewoon bij de Volkswagen-garage.

U kunt er voor van alles terecht: een kleine onderhoudsbeurt, een nieuwe uitlaat of voor een APK-keuring.

Een afspraak maken is niet nodig. Zodra er is vastgesteld wat er moet gebeuren, krijgt u direct een vaste prijsopgave. Dat voorkomt onaangename verrassingen achteraf.

Daarna gaan onze monteurs meteen aan de slag.

Dat zijn trouwens geen doorsnee-monteurs. Voordat ze uw Volkswagen mogen repareren, moeten ze eerst naar school. De Volkswagen-school.

Waar ze alles leren over de 6.843 onderdelen die er in een Volkswagen zitten.

Vanzelfsprekend gebruiken we alleen originele onderdelen. Die stuk voor stuk getest zijn. En waarop u 1 jaar garantie krijgt.

Wat de wachttijd betreft, daar kan nog wel wat vanaf. Al zullen we wel nooit onder de 10,6 seconden komen.

Ach, u heeft tenminste tijd om een kopje koffie te drinken.

En dat hebben we Alain Prost nooit zien doen.

De Volkswagen-garage. Wie anders?

c.
The Volkswagen pit stop:
23 minutes and 17 seconds.
Lotus, McLaren and Ferrari may
laugh. But we are proud of it.
At McLaren, for example, they
don't install a radio during pit
stops. Or fit a sun roof. But
that's completely normal
practice at our pit stops.

a.

b.

c.

Print
Home/
Garden Appliances and Furniture
p.52/53

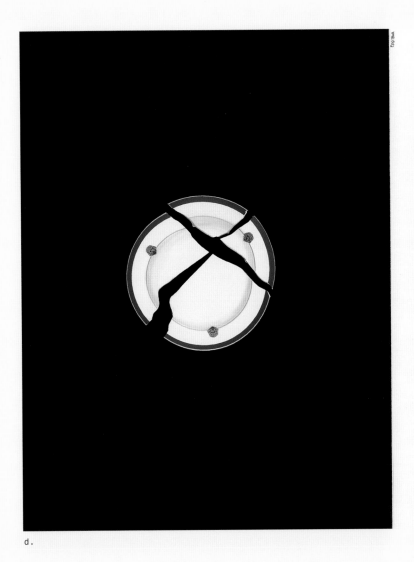

d.

If something goes wrong in your marriage,
you can always replace it.

18 VA 24
VISTA ALEGRE
PORTUGAL

a,b.

Cow
Wood
Advertising Agency
Delvico Bates Barcelona
Client
Balay
Creative Director
Toni Segarra/
Félix Fernandez de Castro
Copywriter
Toni Segarra/Antonio Gómez
Art Director
David Caballero
Photographer
Jané & Osés
Account Supervisor
Lluís Cuesta
Advertiser's Supervisor
Arturo Ballén

c.

Ice
Advertising Agency
Delvico Bates Barcelona
Client
Balay
Creative Director
Toni Segarra/
Félix Fernandez de Castro
Copywriter
Toni Segarra/Antonio Gómez
Art Director
David Caballero
Photographer
Jaime Malé
Account Supervisor
Lluís Cuesta
Advertiser's Supervisor
Arturo Ballén

d.

Broken
Advertising Agency
EPG.TBWA, Lisbon
Client
Vista Alegre
Creative Director
Pedro Bidarra
Copywriter
Pedro Bidarra
Art Director
José Heitor
Account Supervisor
Paulo Renato Melo
Advertiser's Supervisor
Carlos Sousa Machado

There's a new suite shop in town.

Hedge End Retail Park, Charles Watts Way, Southampton.

MULTIYORK

a.

Have we got a couch for you.

So many sofas, you won't believe your eyes.

MULTIYORK

b.

a,b.
There's A New Suite Shop In Town
Have We Got A Couch For You
Advertising Agency
McCann-Erickson Manchester
Client
Multiyork
Creative Director
Keith Ravenscroft
Copywriter
Neil Lancaster
Art Director
David Price
Account Supervisor
Geoff Harris
Advertiser's Supervisor
Rachel Ray

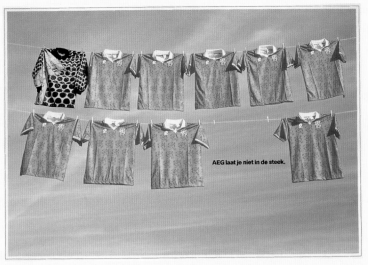

- Tiens, j'ai essayé ta nouvelle découpeuse ce matin.

AEG laat je niet in de steek.

Le béton, l'acier, la pierre, le grès, les tubes en fonte, le fer... Comme vous l'avez compris la découpeuse à disque STIHL TS 460 découpe tout ce qui est découpable et ce, avec le même disque. Son design compact abrite une technique sans précédent... Jugez plutôt : carter moteur en alliage de magnésium pour résister aux vibrations et aux chocs. Allumage électronique digital étanche à 100% facilitant les démarrages et évitant les surrégimes. Un système de filtration à trois étages pour épurer l'air de toutes les poussières même les plus fines... Côté pratique la découpeuse STIHL TS 460 s'utilise aussi aisément sur son chariot de guidage qu'à la main. Sur le plan de la sécurité, le groupe de commande du moteur intégré à lapoignée permet d'actionner d'une seule main la gachette des gaz et son blocage, alors que le pouce peut agir librement sur le contacteur "départ-marche-arrêt". Mais votre revendeur STIHL vous expliquera tout cela très bien. Pour connaître le vôtre, appelez vite au numéro vert suivant.

Appel gratuit

STIHL®
LA PERFORMANCE EST NOTRE EXIGENCE.

c.
AEG never lets you down.
This ad was placed one day after
Ruud Gullit left the National
Dutch football team just before
the World Championships.

d.
"Hey, I tried out your new cutter
this morning."

"At last a camera that can cope with whatever you throw at it."

a.

a.
Ivana Trump
Advertising Agency
Lowe Howard-Spink, London
Client
Olympus
Creative Director
Paul Weinberger
Copywriter
Geoff Cousins
Art Director
Kevin Jones
Photographer
Richard Young/Gavin Cottrell
Account Supervisor
Jeremy Bowles
Communications Director
Ian Dickens

b,c.
Dog
Snail
Advertising Agency
Bartle Bogle Hegarty, London
Client
Sony (UK)
Creative Director
Steve Hooper/Dennis Lewis
Copywriter
Roger Beckett
Art Director
Andy Smart
Photographer
Mark Polyblank
Illustrator
Andy Smart
Account Supervisor
Oliver Lewis-Barclay
Advertiser's Supervisor
Brenda Jones

b.

c.

Roken schaadt de gezondheid. Het kan longkanker of hartklachten veroorzaken. Kon. besluit van 29.4.1981, Stb. 329.

a.

Print
Gift, Luxury Items and Tobacco/
Home Electronics and
Audio-Visual
p.58/59

a.
Unplugged
Advertising Agency
FHV/BBDO, Amstelveen
Client
Douwe Egberts Van Nelle
Tabaksmaatschappij
Copywriter
Marieke Mooijen
Art Director
Jan Paul Rey/Koeweiden Postma
Photographer
Yani

b.
Evolution
Advertising Agency
FHV/BBDO, Amstelveen
Client
Douwe Egberts Van Nelle
Tabaksmaatschappij
Copywriter
David Snellenberg
Art Director
Richard van der Laken/
Sander Bakker/Koeweiden Postma
Photographer
Yani

c.
Slim Thanks
Advertising Agency
Jung von Matt Werbeagentur,
Hamburg
Client
Minolta
Creative Director
Hartwig Keuntje
Copywriter
Mathias Jahn
Art Director
Ove Gley
Photographer
Antonina Gern
Account Supervisor
Dominik Philipp
Advertiser's Supervisor
Ludwig Venhaus

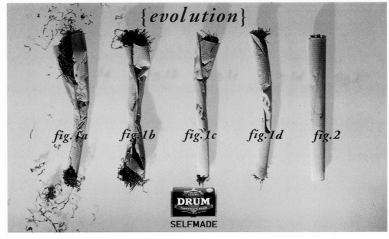

{evolution}

fig.1a   fig.1b   fig.1c   fig.1d   fig.2

DRUM
SELFMADE

Roken schaadt de gezondheid. Het kan longkanker of hartklachten veroorzaken. Kon. besluit van 29.4.1981, Stb. 329.

b.

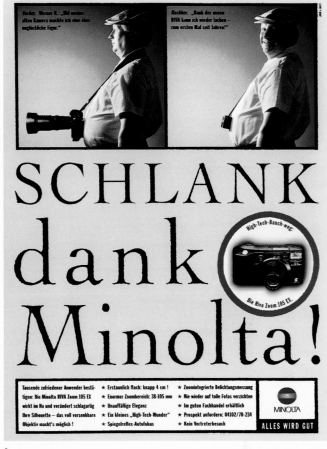

c.
Slim thanks Minolta.

d.
Vertical Grip
Advertising Agency
**Jung von Matt Werbeagentur,
Hamburg**
Client
Minolta
Creative Director
Hartwig Keuntje
Copywriter
Mathias Jahn
Art Director
Ove Gley
Photographer
Stephan Försterling
Account Supervisor
Dominik Philipp
Advertiser's Supervisor
Ludwig Venhaus

d.
In cases like these the new
Dynax 700si has a vertical grip

7mg TAR 0·7mg NICOTINE
SMOKING CAUSES FATAL DISEASES
Health Departments' Chief Medical Officers

a.
Also finalist in the Photography
Category

7mg TAR 0·7mg NICOTINE
PROTECT CHILDREN: DON'T MAKE THEM BREATHE YOUR SMOKE
Health Departments' Chief Medical Officers

b.

7mg TAR 0·7mg NICOTINE
SMOKING CAUSES CANCER
Health Departments' Chief Medical Officers

c.

Print
Gift, Luxury Items and Tobacco
Items
p.60/61

a.
Eurobest Award Winner
Director's Chair
Advertising Agency
Saatchi & Saatchi, London
Client
Gallaher Tobacco
Creative Director
Alexandra Taylor
Copywriter
John Messum/Paul Akins
Art Director
Alexandra Taylor
Photographer
Humberto Rivas
Account Supervisor
Moray MacLennan

d.

And of course now I've got my
waterproof Breitling, it's
stopped raining.

e.

Damn, if I wear my gloves,
no-one will see my Breitling.

b.

Eurobest Award Winner
Phone
Advertising Agency
Saatchi & Saatchi, London
Client
Gallaher Tobacco
Creative Director
Alexandra Taylor
Copywriter
Jason Fretwell
Art Director
Nikolas Studzinski
Photographer
Barney Edwards
Account Supervisor
Tim Duffy

c.

Handbag
Advertising Agency
Saatchi & Saatchi, London
Client
Gallaher Tobacco
Creative Director
Alexandra Taylor
Copywriter
Eugene Ruane
Art Director
Casey Grady
Photographer
Satoshi Saikusa
Account Supervisor
Moray MacLennan

d.

Waterproof
Advertising Agency
DDB Needham France, Paris
Client
Breitling
Creative Director
Bernard Serf/Philippe Rouby
Copywriter
Catherine Castel
Art Director
François Lacheze
Account Supervisor
Michel Niarquin
Advertiser's Supervisor
Benjamin Pardo/
Martine Abihssira

e.

Gloves
Advertising Agency
DDB Needham France, Paris
Client
Breitling
Creative Director
Bernard Serf/Philippe Rouby
Copywriter
Catherine Castel
Art Director
François Lacheze
Account Supervisor
Michel Niarquin
Advertiser's Supervisor
Benjamin Pardo

a.

b.

c.
Torso
Advertising Agency
DMB&B, Hamburg
Client
Lego
Creative Director
Mario Baier
Copywriter
Oliver Dahl
Art Director
Lutz Bühner/Florian Puls
Photographer
Stefan Buechner
Account Supervisor
Dieter Georgi/Gernot Beyer

a,b.
It's Not Necessary To Wait For
The Sales...
There Are Still Schools...
Advertising Agency
Contrapunto, Madrid
Client
Karate School
Creative Director
**Juan Mariano Mancebo/
Ana Hidalgo**
Copywriter
Julio Wallovits
Art Director
Jorge Lopez

a.
Because we couldn't reduce your
paper, we decided to widen our
seat.

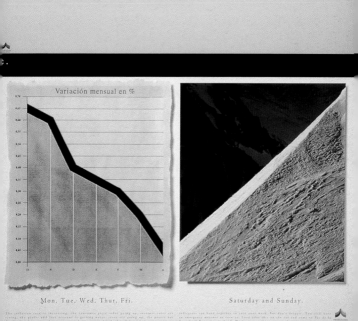

Variación mensual en %

a.
Glamour. There are enough magaz-
ines in which the skies are
always blue, the beaches pearly

b.
Dreams. There are enough magaz-
ines in which women wear
strapless gowns. And Mr Right

c.
Beauty. There are enough magaz-
ines in which the ravages of
time do not exist and your body

Love me or leave me, stranger.

Noen ganger er det fint å kunne dra videre.

InterRail

...ed InterRail-billett i bagasjen er du fri som fuglen i hele Europa. Skulle du plutselig få lyst til å reise videre, går det alltid et tog. Nå kan du både kjøpe InterRail som gjelder hele Europa, og InterRail som gjelder deler av Europa. "Hele Europa" koster i sommer kr 2550.

A special room for you lovebirds.

Noen ganger er det fint å kunne dra videre.

InterRail

GRATIS CARPOOL-SET VAN DE TELEGRAAF.

De Telegraaf
DE KRANT VAN WAKKER NEDERLAND

a.
Free carpool-set from De Telegraaf.
>This was released when Holland's first carpool lane was opened and only cars with 3 or more people in them were allowed in the lane.

RIGHT NOW

WHITES AND BLACKS

IN SOUTH AFRICA

HAVE THE SAME RIGHTS

PROVIDED THAT

THE BLACKS DON'T GO NEAR

WHITE BUILDINGS,

WHITE BUSES,

WHITE BARS,

WHITE BEACHES,

d.

RIGHT NOW

WHITES AND BLACKS

IN SOUTH AFRICA

HAVE THE SAME RIGHTS

ELECTIONS IN
SOUTH AFRICA

From the 21 to the 27 of april on all news reports.
Ramón Tamames and José Miguel Azpiroz
from Johannesburg on Cope Radio.
Because it seems it was true
the world is changing

 COPE

What you listen to

e.

Open your eyes

The
Economist

Truth

hurts

The Economist

b.

If our kitchens aren't spotless, we know where to point the finger.

We could use stainless steel with a less shiny finish for the work surfaces and for the equipment in McDonald's kitchens.

It shows the marks less well.

Instead, we use stainless steel with a shinier finish like the one shown here, which shows up any speck of grease.

In some places, we use a mirror finish which is even less forgiving.

The lighting in our kitchens is much brighter than the rules require, so that there are no dark corners where dirt can hide.

In that respect, we make life really difficult for ourselves.

But we know our kitchens are clean.

And whenever you come into McDonald's you can see they're clean, because you can see our kitchens.

There's nothing quite like a McDonald's.

a.

Fresh from the farm.

There's nothing quite like a McDonald's.

b.

c.

d.

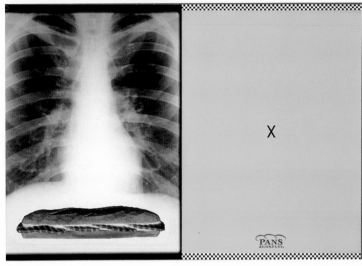

e.

a,b.
Steel
Water
Advertising Agency
Leo Burnett, London
Client
McDonald's Restaurants
Creative Director
Giles Keeble
Copywriter
Richard Cook
Art Director
Jonathan Hall
Photographer
Martin Thompson
Account Supervisor
Christine Clancey
Advertiser's Supervisor

c.
Fire Hose
Advertising Agency
Delvico Bates Barcelona
Client
Agrolimen
Creative Director
Toni Segarra/
Félix Fernandez de Castro
Copywriter
Toni Segarra
Art Director
David Caballero
Photographer
Ramón Serrano
Account Supervisor
Javier Bernal
Advertiser's Supervisor
Josep Maria Bas

d.
Joe Sedelmaier
Advertising Agency
Hermann Vaske, Hamburg
Client
Lürzer's Archive
Creative Director
Hermann Vaske
Art Director
Joe Sedelmaier/Tommie Pinnow
Account Supervisor
Michael Weinzettl
Advertiser's Supervisor
Walter Lürzer

e.
X Ray
Advertising Agency
Delvico Bates Barcelona
Client
Pans & Company
Creative Director
David Caballero/
Toni Segarra/
Félix Fernandez de Castro
Copywriter
David Caballero
Art Director
David Caballero
Photographer
Marcus Welby
Account Supervisor
Javier Bernal

YOU'LL BE CARRYING HIM FOR THE NEXT 18 YEARS.

He's only 6 months old and he's already getting through money like water.

In fact, even before his birth, Oliver here had clocked up £1,000 in baby equipment, clothes and toiletries.

And over the next 18 years he could chomp through mum and dad's finances to the tune of well over £100,000. That's why, when you have a baby, it is never too early to make plans.

You could start by having a chat with our financial advisers. They can ease the burden with simple yet sound advice.

They might suggest you put some money aside to cover school fees, for example. (Five years at a private school can cost a whopping £30,000.)

Our financial advisers will also help you protect your family.

So you can choose the right life assurance plan, as well as the best insurance scheme to cover your home and valuables.

Because apart from wanting to eat everything from the hi-fi to your porcelain, bouncing babies don't much care what they bounce into.

Pop into your local Halifax branch to arrange an appointment with an adviser, or call us free on 0800 10 11 10.

FINANCIAL PLANNING FOR YOUNG FAMILIES. **HALIFAX** OUR EXPERTISE IS UNDERSTANDABLE.

a.

WHEN YOU RETIRE, LET YOUR HAIR DOWN.

FINANCIAL PLANNING FOR RETIREMENT. **HALIFAX** OUR EXPERTISE IS UNDERSTANDABLE.

b.

SHOCK YOUR PARENTS ONE LAST TIME.

PENSIONS

FINANCIAL PLANNING FOR YOUNG PEOPLE **HALIFAX** OUR EXPERTISE IS UNDERSTANDABLE.

c.

Print
Banking, Financial and Insurance
p.74/75

HE USED TO BE A LITTLE DEAR. NOW HE'S A LITTLE EXPENSIVE.

As your kids grow, so do their running costs.

Just keeping them in wheels could saddle you with bills running into the thousands.

Then there are all the little extras your little darlings will demand.

Take clothes for example. What they're desperate to wear this year, they won't be seen dead in next.

Which is why the sooner you get on your bike (or his) and get down to the Halifax, the better.

Our financial advisers can help you plan for the best of times as well as the worst.

We could sort you out with a tailor-made investment plan, so you'll have a lump sum to set against those large bills. Or we might recommend a school fees plan to take the pain out of putting them through school or college.

And even if the thought of them leaving home makes you reach for your hanky, you'd be better off thinking about it now.

A chat with our pensions adviser could ensure that when the kids finally hand in their 'L' plates and depart, you'll be left with plenty of money to spend on yourself.

How about a motorbike of your own?

Drop into your local Halifax branch to arrange an appointment, or call us free on 0800 10 11 10.

FINANCIAL PLANNING FOR FAMILIES. **HALIFAX** OUR EXPERTISE IS UNDERSTANDABLE.

d.

a.	b.	c.	d.
Oliver	Waterskier	Peter	Bikes
Advertising Agency	Advertising Agency	Advertising Agency	Advertising Agency
DFSD Bozell, London	**DFSD Bozell, London**	**DFSD Bozell, London**	**DFSD Bozell, London**
Client	Client	Client	Client
Halifax Financial Services	**Halifax Financial Services**	**Halifax Financial Services**	**Halifax Financial Services**
Creative Director	Creative Director	Creative Director	Creative Director
Greg Delaney/Brian Stewart	**Greg Delaney/Brian Stewart**	**Greg Delaney/Brian Stewart**	**Greg Delaney/Brian Stewart**
Copywriter	Copywriter	Copywriter	Copywriter
Mike McKenna	**David Alexander**	**David Alexander**	**Greg Delaney**
Art Director	Art Director	Art Director	Art Director
Dave Dye	**Sue Lamb**	**Rob Fletcher**	**Gareth Pitman**
Photographer	Photographer	Photographer	Photographer
Malcolm Venville	**David Stewart**	**Malcolm Venville**	**David Stewart**
Account Supervisor	Account Supervisor	Account Supervisor	Account Supervisor
Mary Leslie	**Mary Leslie**	**Mary Leslie**	**Mary Leslie**
Advertiser's Supervisor	Advertiser's Supervisor	Advertiser's Supervisor	Advertiser's Supervisor
Steve McDermott	**Steve McDermott**	**Steve McDermott**	**Steve McDermott**

Vous comparez le prix
des lessives au centime
près, alors pourquoi
laissez-vous de l'argent
dormir sur un compte
qui rapporte 0 % ?

CAISSE D'EPARGNE

a.
You compare washing powder
prices down to the last penny,
so why do you let your money
sleep in an account which gives
you nothing?

b.

a.
Lessive
Advertising Agency
BDDP, Boulogne
Client
Caisse D'Epargne
Creative Director
Marie-Catherine Dupuy/
Jean-Pierre Barbou
Copywriter
Olivier Altman
Art Director
Robin De Lestrade
Photographer
Philippe Pollet Villard
Account Supervisor
Louis Maria
Advertiser's Supervisor
Alain Margerit

b,c.
Old Man
Nose & Ears
Advertising Agency
Bartle Bogle Hegarty, London
Client
National Westminster Bank
Creative Director
Steve Hooper/Dennis Lewis
Copywriter
Paul Silburn
Art Director
Tiger Savage
Photographer
Malcolm Venville
Account Supervisor
Emma Rea
Advertiser's Supervisor
Jo Veale

So you've **got your moth**er's nose
and your **father's ears. At** least you can
have **yo**ur **own bank** account.

A NatWest Card Plus account has its own unique distinguishing features.
Like a Cashcard, and access to over 6,000 cash machines. If you had one it would really make you look good.

♻ **National Westminster Bank**
We're here to make life easier

Just as easy to use for small purchases as it is for large ones.

VISA. PERFECT FOR THAT NOT-SO-SPECIAL OCCASION.

VISA

MAKING LIFE EASIER.

a.

Print
Banking, Financial and Insurance
p.78/79

a.
Ring
Advertising Agency
Saatchi & Saatchi, London
Client
Visa Worldwide
Creative Director
James Lowther/Simon Dicketts
Copywriter
Mary Wear
Art Director
Damon Collins
Photographer
Daniel Jouanneau
Account Supervisor
John Rudaizky
Advertiser's Supervisor
Mark Giffen

b,c.
Kittens
Back Of The Head
Advertising Agency
Saatchi & Saatchi, London
Client
Visa Worldwide
Creative Director
James Lowther/Simon Dicketts
Copywriter
Mary Wear
Art Director
Damon Collins
Photographer
Paul Bussell
Account Supervisor
John Rudaizky
Advertiser's Supervisor
Mark Giffen

**YOU RAN OUT OF CASH
IN THE SUPERMARKET.
WHAT ARE YOU, A MONSTER?**

VISA

MAKING LIFE EASIER.

**YOU'VE BEEN STARING AT
IT FOR TEN MINUTES.
ARE YOU A HAIRDRESSER,
OR IN A BANK QUEUE?**

VISA

MAKING LIFE EASIER.

EN? WANNEER GAAN WE NAAR DE OPTICIEN?

ZONDER DAT U ER METEEN IETS VAN MERKT, KUNNEN UW OGEN ACHTERUIT GAAN. EENS PER JAAR EEN OOGCONTROLE IS DUS ECHT NIET OVERDREVEN. STICHTING BETER ZIEN.

a.

EN? WANNEER GAAN WE NAAR DE OPTICIEN?

ZONDER DAT U ER METEEN IETS VAN MERKT, KUNNEN UW OGEN ACHTERUIT GAAN. EENS PER JAAR EEN OOGCONTROLE IS DUS ECHT NIET OVERDREVEN. STICHTING BETER ZIEN.

b.

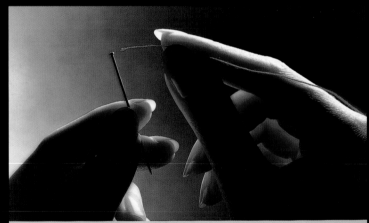

EN? WANNEER GAAN WE NAAR DE OPTICIEN?

ZONDER DAT U ER METEEN IETS VAN MERKT, KUNNEN UW OGEN ACHTERUIT GAAN. EENS PER JAAR EEN OOGCONTROLE IS DUS ECHT NIET OVERDREVEN. STICHTING BETER ZIEN.

c.

Print
Commercial Public Services

EN? WANNEER GAAN WE NAAR DE OPTICIEN?

ZONDER DAT U ER METEEN IETS VAN MERKT, KUNNEN UW OGEN ACHTERUIT GAAN. EENS PER JAAR EEN OOGCONTROLE IS DUS ECHT NIET OVERDREVEN. STICHTING BETER ZIEN.

d.
So. Isn't it about time you saw
the optician?

a,b,c,d.
Deodorant
Stamp
Pin
Microwave Oven
Advertising Agency
Campaign Company, Amsterdam
Client
Stichting Beter Zien
Copywriter
Lysbeth Bijlstra
Art Director
Diederick Hillenius
Photographer
Paul Ruigrok
Account Supervisor
Mechteld Snouck

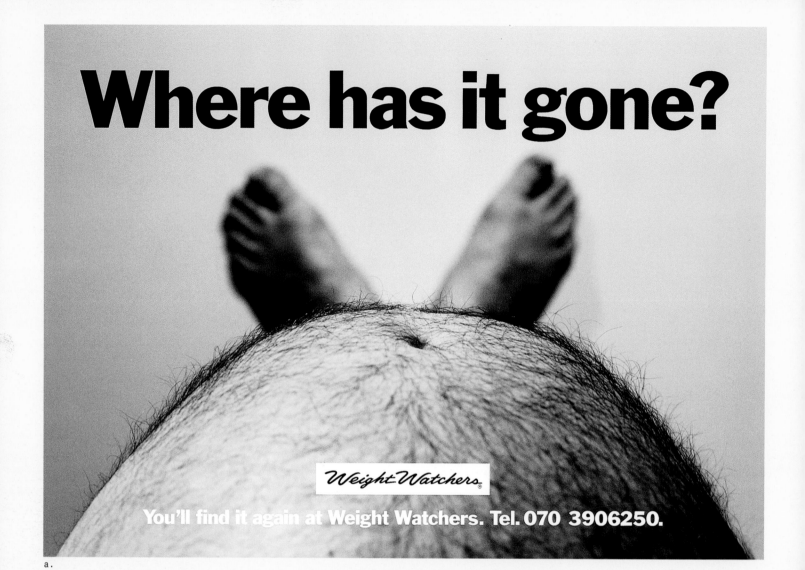

a.

If you feel ashamed about show-ing your two breasts, imagine showing just one.

b.

c.

a.

WHO SAYS ETHNIC MINORITIES CAN'T GET JOBS? THERE ARE OPENINGS EVERYWHERE.

Lavatory attendant. Office cleaner. Somebody has to do all the low-paid, menial jobs, but why is it so often people from ethnic minorities? Prejudice, racial discrimination and harassment are denying people the choice of job they deserve. It's unjust and unfair. More than that, it's a terrible waste of British talent.

a.

b.

CRIMINAL ISN'T IT?

A 1992 survey of Midlands crown courts revealed that some ethnic minorities are receiving longer prison sentences. On average, up to 9 months longer than white people for the same crimes. If this is typical, it leads to one simple and rather alarming conclusion.

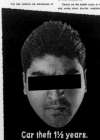

Car theft 9 months.   Car theft 1½ years.

b.

c.

AND YOU GET ANNOYED ABOUT JUNK MAIL.

Imagine going to your door and finding, there, on the mat, not bills, or a paper, or junk mail, but pieces of dog excrement. As you stare, shocked, a heavy boot kicks the door. Hateful voices outside scream obscenities, telling you to get out, threatening your family. Why are they persecuting you? When will they stop?

c.

d.

CHILDREN FROM ETHNIC MINORITIES OFTEN GET THE WORST MARKS AT SCHOOL.

Actually, studies show that some ethnic minorities get the best grades at school. But of course, you won't have heard about that. All you will have heard about are the kind of marks that grab the headlines. The vicious playground beatings, the horrific knife attacks and the senseless murders.

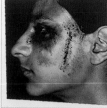
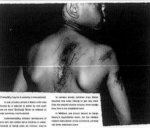

d.

Print
Non-Commercial Public Services
and Political Advertising
p.84/85

a.
Openings
Advertising Agency
Saatchi & Saatchi, London
Client
Commission for Racial Equality
Creative Director
James Lowther/Simon Dicketts
Copywriter
Ajab Samrai Singh/
Giles Montgomery
Art Director
Ajab Samrai Singh
Photographer
John Turner
Account Supervisor
Charles Fallon
Advertiser's Supervisor
Marjorie Thompson

THERE ARE LOTS OF PLACES IN BRITAIN WHERE RACISM DOESN'T EXIST.

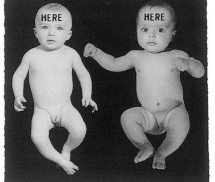

In so many ways Britain is a racist country. In 1993 alone the police recorded over 9,000 incidents of racial harassment, abuse, assault, arson and murder. Thousands more incidents go unreported. As many as 120,000 a year, according to the Home Office. Worryingly, even this is still only half the problem.

Aside from the ugly, violent, obvious incidents of racism there's something that's perhaps even more disturbing.

The not-so-obvious incidents.

Black people are stopped by the police four times as often as white people. Other minorities receive up to ten times as many job rejections as white people.

And a recent investigation revealed that Asian women are twice as likely to be unemployed as white women, even if they possess better qualifications.

It's hard for most people to appreciate the extent of discrimination in Britain.

But anyone can appreciate this: it isn't just hurtful or morally wrong.

It's wrong for all kinds of reasons.

Britain needs all the best scientists, nurses, doctors, police officers, teachers and business brains it can muster.

We can't afford to squander anyone's talents, whatever colour their skin is.

And yet, racial discrimination makes us do just that. How can we rid ourselves of something that's so ingrained in our society?

There is hope.

It lies in all the places in Britain where racism and prejudice simply don't exist.

In the minds of babies.

People aren't born hating each other, they just grow up that way.

But the next generation doesn't have to.

They could grow up in a society which accepts and treats everyone as equals.

Who knows? Maybe their children will only hear about racism in history lessons.

For a start, shouldn't parents of all races teach their children that racism is wrong? And then back up that teaching by setting a good example themselves.

If you're a witness to any kind of racist incident (or indeed, if you're a victim of one) report it to the police.

If you find a newspaper article or a radio or TV programme racially offensive, write to the people who made it and tell them so. Write to the Press Complaints Commission, the Radio Authority or the Independent Television Commission.

It's worth knowing that in many cases racial discrimination is more than unfair, it's downright unlawful.

The Race Relations Act was passed as long ago as 1976.

It states simply that people should not be discriminated against on the grounds of colour, race, ethnic origin or nationality.

The Act could be used to great and good effect, if only people were a little less ready to dismiss it as 'politically correct' bureaucracy. (After all, why be prejudiced against a law against prejudice?)

The Act says all children are entitled to an education free of discrimination.

But not every school provides one.

And not every school is doing as much as they could to stamp out racial bullying among children.

Local Education Authorities, governors and even individual teachers all have a duty to help uphold the law.

The Act also states that employers shouldn't discriminate against workers or job applicants because of colour or race.

Companies are encouraged to draw up equal opportunity policies. Some do and carry on discriminating anyway.

If there's discrimination at work talk to your Trade Union about it. You could also speak to your local Citizens Advice Bureau or Racial Equality Council (both of which are listed in the phone book).

If you're concerned about race issues of any kind, you could write to your MP.

Or you could write to us.

The Commission for Racial Equality was set up by the Race Relations Act.

We're an independent body funded by an annual Home Office grant.

One of our duties is to draw attention to discrimination wherever it occurs. To this end, we investigate areas of discrimination and produce reports of our findings (some of which make quite disturbing reading).

Another of our duties is to monitor how the Act is working. We champion important test cases through the courts, which may lead to changes in the law.

We also offer guidelines to the police, Education Authorities and employers on how to provide equal opportunities.

What we don't do is tell companies they must employ so many minorities or else.

So-called 'positive' discrimination is the same as any other kind of discrimination.

The fact is, most of our work involves fighting the serious, day-in day-out inter-racial discrimination that has no place in a civilised, democratic country.

Indeed, perhaps the most important of the objectives that we are working towards is the elimination of all such discrimination.

It won't be easy.

Hating others because they're different seems childish.

But that's an insult to children.

So, for all our advances, maybe it's time we took one giant leap backwards.

To the open, tolerant state of mind we had when we were born.

For a list of our reports, guides, posters and leaflets send a stamped, self-addressed A4 envelope to: CRE Information Section, Elliot House, 10-12 Allington St, London SW1E 5EH.

COMMISSION FOR RACIAL EQUALITY

---

b.

Criminal

Advertising Agency
Saatchi & Saatchi, London
Client
Commission for Racial Equality
Creative Director
James Lowther/Simon Dicketts
Copywriter
Ajab Samrai Singh
Art Director
Ajab Samrai Singh
Photographer
Tim O'Sullivan/Alistair Thane
Account Supervisor
Charles Fallon
Advertiser's Supervisor
Marjorie Thompson

c.

Junk Mail

Advertising Agency
Saatchi & Saatchi, London
Client
Commission for Racial Equality
Creative Director
James Lowther/Simon Dicketts
Copywriter
Ajab Samrai Singh
Art Director
Ajab Samrai Singh
Photographer
John Turner
Account Supervisor
Charles Fallon
Advertiser's Supervisor
Marjorie Thompson

d.

Education

Advertising Agency
Saatchi & Saatchi, London
Client
Commission for Racial Equality
Creative Director
James Lowther/Simon Dicketts
Copywriter
Ajab Samrai Singh/Chris Kirk
Art Director
Ajab Samrai Singh
Photographer
Barry Lategan
Account Supervisor
Charles Fallon
Advertiser's Supervisor
Marjorie Thompson

e.

Babies

Advertising Agency
Saatchi & Saatchi, London
Client
Commission for Racial Equality
Creative Director
James Lowther/Simon Dicketts
Copywriter
Ajab Samrai Singh
Art Director
Ajab Samrai Singh
Photographer
Alaistair Thane
Account Supervisor
Charles Fallon
Advertiser's Supervisor
Marjorie Thompson

Les premiers temps, ce n'est peut-être pas plus mal qu'il y ait
un peu de distance entre lui et vous (par exemple 0,07mm).

Une rupture c'est toujours difficile. Se retrouver seule quand on avait l'habitude d'être deux,
ce n'est pas marrant. Bien sûr il y a les copines. Bien sûr, tout le monde est gentil, attentif.

N'empêche: se retrouver invitée à un dîner où il n'y a que des couples, ce n'est pas simple.
Et en même temps on n'a pas vraiment le cœur à cuisiner pour soi toute seule. "Bonjour
Monsieur le Boucher, je voudrais un steak pour une", ça sonne bizarrement.

Et puis -cela prend le temps que cela prend- on finit par faire son deuil de ce qui avait
tant compté. On sent qu'autre chose peut recommencer.

Et à ce moment-là, ce ne sont ni les candidats qui manquent, ni les risques.

D'abord, parce qu'on ne sait pas exactement ce qu'on cherche: se rassurer? S'abandonner
un peu? L'homme de sa vie? Et qu'est-ce qui prouve que le premier sera le bon?

Rien, à vrai dire. Et c'est justement parce que nous voulons pouvoir nous chercher, nous
tromper ou simplement nous consoler que le préservatif a son utilité.

D'accord, dans ces moments-là, ce que l'on a en tête, ce n'est pas se protéger du sida.
D'accord, le préservatif, ce n'est pas facile quand on n'a pas eu l'habitude de l'utiliser.

Mais tout de même: cette liberté toute neuve, vous ne voudriez pas la perdre alors que
vous venez à peine de la gagner?

Agence de Prévention du Sida

Si vous souhaitez plus d'informations, écrivez à l'Agence de Prévention du Sida, rue de Haerne, 42 - 1040 Bruxelles - 02/627 75 11

Le préservatif. On préférerait faire sans, mais on est bien obligé de faire avec.

a.
At the beginning, it wouldn't
be a bad thing to keep a little
distance between you and him
(for example 0.07mm).

a.
Distance
Advertising Agency
LHHS, Brussels
Client
Agence de Prevention SIDA
Creative Director
Anouk Sendrowicz/Eric Hollander
Copywriter
Eric Hollander
Art Director
Anouk Sendrowicz/
Olivier Steenuit
Photographer
Hughes De Wurstenberger
Account Supervisor
Isabelle Moulart
Advertiser's Supervisor
Vincent Magos/Patrick Petitjean

b.
Famous
Advertising Agency
Delvico Bates Barcelona
Client
Spanish Cancer Association
(AECC)
Creative Director
Toni Segarra/
Félix Fernandez de Castro
Copywriter
Javier Carro
Art Director
David Caballero/Enric Aguilera
Photographer
Ibid
Account Supervisor
Marta Turón

c.
Drugs
Advertising Agency
Nova Publicidade, Lisbon
Client
AMI
Creative Director
José Ricardo Cabaço/
Eduardo Martins
Copywriter
Judite Mota
Art Director
Pedro Ferreira
Photographer
Gillian Campbell
Account Supervisor
Manuel Rendeiro

Print
Charitable Causes
p.86/87

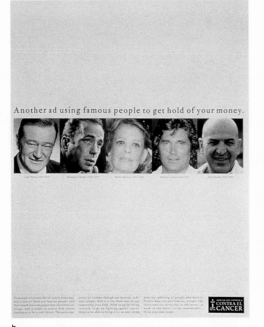
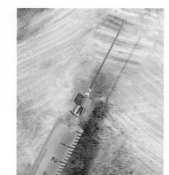

DO YOU SUSPECT THAT SOMETIMES PEOPLE BEG FOR MONEY TO BUY DRUGS ?

THIS IS ONE OF THOSE TIMES.

This time you can be sure: the money you give us will be used to buy drugs capable of caring hundreds of patients at AMI missions around the world. AMI - International Medical Assistence - only subsists upon donations and the action of volunteers that go to the most needfull places in the world to give people medical assistance. They help victims of wars, natural catastrophies or underdevelopment. You too, can volunteer even if it is with only some money. And you can be sure it will be used for a good cause.

Assistência Médica Internacional. Give some money. It won't hurt you.

Rua José do Patrocínio n° 49 - Marvila 1900 - Lisboa - Portugal.   Transferência Bancária para a conta n° 0007 0015 0027781 0009 79 do BES.

c.

FAITES QU'UN JOUR NOTRE JOURNAL DISPARAISSE. ACHETEZ LE.

MACADAM JOURNAL

REJOINDRE LE MONDE   Le journal vendu par les sans domicile fixe.

d.

Make our newspaper disappear.
Buy it. The newspaper sold by
the homeless.

d.
Macadam Journal
Advertising Agency
BCRC, Paris
Client
Macadam Journal
Creative Director
Pascal Gregoire
Copywriter
Olivier Moine
Art Director
Peggy Mocquay

a.
To get the same quality printing
as an Epson, you really need to
have faith.

c.
To retrieve lost dogs call the
RSPCA, to retrieve badly printed
dogs call Epson.

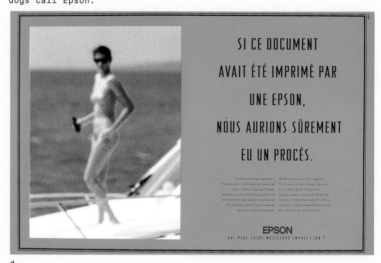

d.
If this had been printed on an
Epson we'd have been taken to
court.

e.
Epson printers would just like
to remind you that the penalty
for counterfeiters under Article
139 is life imprisonment.

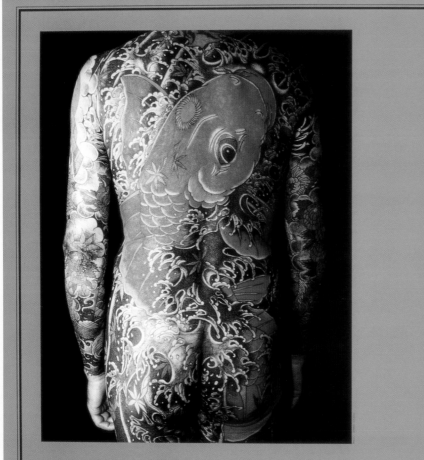

CE QU'UNE MAIN
PEUT FAIRE À VOTRE DOS,
UNE IMPRIMANTE
EPSON PEUT
LE FAIRE À UNE FEUILLE
DE PAPIER.

EPSON

QUI PEUT FAIRE MEILLEURE IMPRESSION ?

b.
What a hand can do to your back,
an Epson printer can do to a
piece of paper.

a,b,c,d,e,f.
Le Parchemin
Tatouage
Dalmatien
Le Nue
La Prison
Advertising Agency
BDDP, Boulogne
Client
Epson
Creative Director
Jean-Claude Jouis
Copywriter
Olivier Altman
Art Director
Robin de Lestrade
Account Supervisor
Thierry Bagnashino
Advertiser's Supervisor
Jérôme Piot

According to research, this man should be a California surfer.

Richard Bradley, Chairman.

Although it pains us to admit it, our research tells us that when many people in the U.K. think of Apple™ computer users, they think of free-spirited, light-hearted individuals. The kind of person you'd find more often on a surfboard than a board of directors.

Not exactly the image that leaps to mind when you look at the loyal (not to mention highly successful) Macintosh™ owner pictured at right.

While it is accurate that Macintosh was originally conceived in the slightly off-centre state of California, it's equally true that today this unconventional invention is the computer of choice for over 10 million lawyers, architects, accountants and other serious business people around the world.

What's so different about a Macintosh?

If there's anything offbeat about Macintosh, it's not the people who use it. It's the concept it's based on.

The Macintosh system began with a very simple, but very revolutionary idea: computers should be for ordinary people. To make both ordinary and extraordinary things easier to do.

From the very first chip, our engineers made things harder on themselves so it would be easier for the people who use Macintosh. Although the computers and software that operate Macintosh have been refined, improved and expanded over the years, the original idea has remained the same.

That's why you'll notice, whenever you use a Macintosh, that there aren't any complicated commands to memorise. No indecipherable computer codes to slow you down.

Which means, of course, you'll spend less time wondering how to do what you need to, and more time actually doing it.

What's in it for you?

How does increased productivity sound for starters?

As all too many people who have bought computers can tell you, the most expensive part of the proposition isn't the computer itself. It's learning to use it. Figuring out how to make it meet your particular needs. Not to mention answering all of those technical questions.

Fortunately, since the Macintosh is designed to anticipate the way people think, you'll find that you simply won't need as much costly training and ongoing technical support[1].

Furthermore, every program you can run on the Macintosh (and there are literally thousands of them) works in the same logical, consistent manner. From Lotus 1-2-3™ to WordPerfect, once you've learned one program, you've learned the basics of them all.

If it sounds easy, it's probably because it is. Which would explain why more than 98.6% of all Macintosh owners are satisfied with their purchases.[2]

Sure, but what does it cost?

With recent price reductions of up to 35%* on selected models, a Macintosh is now more affordable than ever. In fact, you can own one for as little as £695**.

When you take into account all of the time and money a Macintosh will save you on computer training and technical support, the price is even more appealing.

The Macintosh Classic™ line offers all the cost-saving benefits of Macintosh for as little as £695. And since that price includes built-in networking and file sharing software (as well as a keyboard, monitor and sound capabilities), you can not only afford to give a Macintosh to all your staff, you can also connect them together so they can work even more efficiently.

The Macintosh PowerBook™ line offers a choice of six models. Twice named a Product of the Year by the likes of Time, Business Week and Fortune, PowerBook has set a new standard among notebook computers for simplicity, display quality and intelligent design. No wonder we sold more than one PowerBook per minute last year.

The Macintosh Quadra™, considered "the ultimate workstation for most users" by BYTE Magazine[3], gives you all the horsepower you need to handle even the most challenging projects. Engineering, drafting and 3-D rendering, as well as huge spreadsheets or book-length publications.

What about your old computer?

Good question.

Although most people don't seem to realise it, every Macintosh built today is designed to work with the MS-DOS™ PCs your business may already have.

Most Macintosh computers incorporate an Apple SuperDrive™ that reads and writes to 3 1/2" MS-DOS formatted disks. Which enables you to easily share information between computers.

And, by adding a program called SoftPC™, you can even run MS-DOS software on a Macintosh.

All of which is a technical way of saying that you can continue to use your old computers once you've bought a Macintosh. Although, we should warn you, you probably won't want to once you've discovered the legendary ease of a Macintosh.

What are you waiting for?

With over 10 million Apple computers currently in use around the world, we can hardly call them a well-kept secret.

However, according to our research department, the advantages of a Macintosh are still relatively undiscovered in the U.K.

If you'd like to find out how you can turn your fellow countrymen's lack of knowledge into your competitive advantage, simply dial 0800 127753.

We'll rush you our free Apple Information Pack — filled with product specifications, comparison studies and other vital facts that show you how a Macintosh can save you time and make you money.

Or, simply fill out the coupon below. We'd love to have your name for our mailing list. Even if it does happen to be Surfer Joe, Hangdog or Wildman.

To receive your free information-filled package, complete the coupon, enclose in an envelope and forward to Ms. Penny Bousfield, Customer Care Administrator, Apple Computer U.K. Limited, Freepost, London SW15 2YY. (No stamp required).

First Name _____
Surname _____
Job title _____
Company name _____
Address _____
City _____
County _____
Postcode _____
Tel -STD(___)

I want information about:

☐ Macintosh in Business
☐ Macintosh in Education
☐ Macintosh at Home

☐ Tick here if you do NOT wish to receive future mailings from Apple

Apple

b.

c.

a.
Here's just a few things to bear
in mind if you're thinking of
applying for a patent yourself.

Print
Other Business to Business
p.92/93

Att söka patent i Asien är inte svårt. Läs själv.

出力側に連結する目的 た太陽歯車を有する遊 歯車の組及び係合遊星歯車より成り、それら歯 が出力軸に連結した遊星歯車担体上に担持され またそれら歯車が輪歯車に係合し、この輪歯車 係合手段によって、前記ハウジングに対する回 に抗して入力軸と出力軸との間で減速比駆動を なうか、或は入力軸及び出力軸に対する回転に して該軸間で直接に駆動を行なうかのいずれか よりロックできる自動車用のレンジギヤボック において、輪歯車（14）が、輪歯車担体の役を る係合スリーブ（18）と回転不能に連結し、且 出力軸（8）に同心的に取付けられ、該輪歯車 出力軸（8）との間に回転不能な連結を作る第

ング（21）に係合し、また他の係合位置において ハウジング（3）に固定された第2係合リング （25）に係合することを特徴とする特許請求の範 囲第1項に記載のレンジギヤボックス。

3）係合リング（21，25）が、互に向い合った 同期円錐体（23，26）で作られ、各々が係合スリ ーブ（18）に係合する個々の同期リング（24，27） と協力することを特徴とする特許請求の範囲第2 項に記載のレンジギヤボックス。

4）同期リング（23，26）の各々が、円錐体の 間に配置された褄状ばね（34）の助けで、そのそ れぞれの同期円錐体（24，27）に対して押圧する ことができ、前記褄状ばねが1つの係合位置にお いて係合スリーブ（18）中の第1内部リング溝

Ring oss. Vi har samarbetspartners över hela världen.

ALBIHNS
FRÅN IDÉ TILL FRAMGÅNG

H. ALBIHNS PATENTBYRÅ AB, STOCKHOLM 08-796 63 00
ALBIHN WEST AB, GÖTEBORG 031-80 62 85
ALBIHN WILLQUIST AB, LINKÖPING 013-12 65 20

HELA EUROPA BEHÖVER FIBRER
TILL FRUKOST.

DET FINNS EN stor marknad att mätta där ute, men också många konkurrerande företag. En konkurrens där storlek och specialisering blir allt viktigare.

Det är därför AssiDomän nu bildas. Vi blir ett av Europas tio största skogsindustriföretag och vi specialiserar oss på produkter där vår färska, svenska träfiber ger störst konkurrensfördelar: sågade trävaror, förpackningsmaterial och förpackningar.

Produkter som de flesta europeiska företag behöver. Det är ett klokt sätt att förvalta både Sveriges skogar och vår egen svenska skogsindustri. Och *dina pengar*, om du väljer att investera dem i AssiDomän-aktier, när bolaget inom kort börsnoteras.

AssiDomän

ASSIDOMÄN-AKTIEN KOMMER ATT ERBJUDAS TILL FÖRSÄLJNING PÅ DE FLESTA BANK- OCH POSTKONTOR FRÅN DEN 9 MARS. **MER INFORMATION PÅ TV4 TEXT-TV SIDAN 190.**

a.

b.
Let's Crack It
Advertising Agency
Lowe & Partners, Frankfurt
Client
Adam Opel
Creative Director
Rolf Greulich
Copywriter
Christiane Boje
Art Director
Anthony Cliff/Hans Warnitz
Photographer
Clive Davis
Account Supervisor
Justus J. Schneider/
Ulrich Seiffert
Advertiser's Supervisor
Markus Hintz/Uwe Braun

a.
Europe Needs Fibres
For Breakfast
Advertising Agency
Alm & Co., Stockholm
Client
Assidomän
Copywriter
Christer Alm
Art Director
Ninna Lindkvist
Account Supervisor
Daniel Berglind/Eva Samuelsson
Advertiser's Supervisor
Berit Hallberg

LASST KNACKEN!

Vom 24.–26. September 1993 findet in Schweden – Heimat des Knäckebrots – das Halbfinale des Davis-Cups statt. Opel als offizieller Sponsor wünscht dem deutschen Team viel Erfolg, begeisternde Matches und den richtigen Biß. **OPEL** ⊖

b.
Let's crack it.

Eugene kissed goodbye to his bus fare,
but like the Murphy's he wasn't bitter.

b.

The Lotto was split 1,062,437 ways,
but like the Murphy's Paddy wasn't bitter.

a.

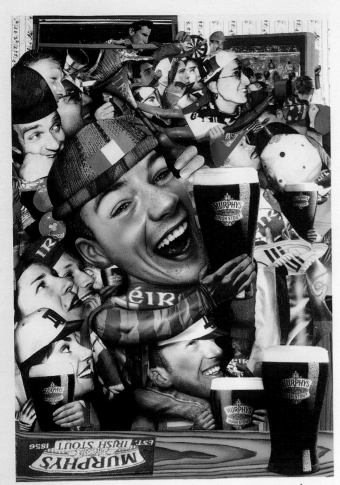

Jack's Boys didn't make it to the final, but like the Murphy's we weren't bitter.

c.

Dehydration was a problem for the boys from Cork, but like the Murphy's they weren't bitter.

d.

a,b,c,d.
Lotto
Blarney Stone
Big Game
Dehydration
Advertising Agency
Bartle Bogle Hegarty, London
Client
The Whitbread Beer Company
Creative Director
John Hegarty
Copywriter
Bruce Crouch
Art Director
Graham Watson
Illustrator
Janet Woolley
Account Supervisor
Paddy Byng
Advertiser's Supervisor
Mike Dowells

Defy the laws of gravity. After all they were invented by a man.

So Sir Isaac Newton
decreed that what goes up
must come down?
(Obviously, the only
working out the guy did
was with a quill.)
Now there is a new set
of physical laws.
They state that a
body in motion = a mind at ease.
Once you've got
your head round that,
anything seems possible.
Go ahead.
Be a law unto yourself.
Just do it.

a.

a.
Gravity
Advertising Agency
Simons Palmer Denton Clemmow and Johnson, London
Client
Nike UK
Creative Director
Andy McKay/Paul Hodgkinson
Copywriter
Paul Silburn
Art Director
Tiger Savage
Photographer
Nadav Kander
Account Supervisor
Clare Dobbie
Advertiser's Supervisor
Tony Hill

Print
Photography
p.98/99

Devon, U.K.

b.

b.
Nude No.6
Advertising Agency
Nadav Kander Photography, London
Client
Nadav Kander Photography
Photographer
Nadav Kander

Eurobest/3 Packaging & Design

The winner is... Aesthetics!
This year's judging for the Eurobest Awards 1994 for Packaging and Design took place in Barcelona.
>Each jury member was briefed on the do's and don't's of judging the entries and the importance of a unique idea, the creativity in execution and the effectiveness in the specific market were the basic criteria.
>The judging started. The judging finished. Aesthetics won again!
>Why is it that every designer falls in love while judging bottles of wines, boxes of cigars or exclusive liquors? Is it the craftsmanship of all these details that every designer admires? Or is it the high class exclusivity that makes the profession of the designer so valuable and artistic? Why is it so difficult for every jury around the world not to award only beautiful bottles and boxes? It is the designer in ourselves who surpasses all the judgement rules and awards craftsmanship. Nobody knows the success of a beautiful wine bottle in the market because the whole market looks beautiful. Nobody can appreciate the innovation in a beautifully designed box because there is no real innovation, only extreme beauty.
>In future, all juries should refuse to give too many awards to "easily made beautiful design" categories. To change the market codes, refresh the shelf or to create consumer loyalty by being different should be the incentive behind future winners. We need courageous clients and convincing designers and excellent designs to achieve this. For this reason I am very glad that a "beautiful!" printed piece of paper wrapped around cheese has been awarded the Grand Prix.
Rob van den Berg
Millford-van den Berg Design

a.

b.

a,b.
Spadel:
Spa Reine Waters
Design Group
Motive Global Design
Consultants, Brussels
Client
Spadel
Designer
Romano Scuvee
Photographer
Romy Tembuyser
Illustrator
Studio T
Account Supervisor
Marie-Lou Scuvee

c.

d.

c.
Harveys Bristol Cream Sherry
Design Group
Blackburn's, London
Client
Harveys of Bristol
Designer
John Blackburn
Creative Director
John Blackburn

d.
Arnold Dettling:
Dettling Kirschwasser
Design Group
Lewis Moberly, London
Client
Arnold Dettling
Designer
Mary Lewis

a.

a.

Eurobest Award Winner

Berry Bros and Rudd:

The Glenrothes Malt Whisky

Design Group

Blackburn's, London

Client

Berry Bros and Rudd

Designer

Belinda Duggan

Creative Director

John Blackburn

b.

Asda Stores:

Hungarian Wines

Design Group

Elmwood, Leeds

Client

Asda Stores

Designer

Gary Swindell

Photographer

Simon Larbalestier

Account Supervisor

Greg Taylor

c.

Harveys of Bristol:

Cockburn's 'Anno' Port

Design Group

Blackburn's, London

Client

Harveys of Bristol

Designer

Belinda Duggan

Creative Director

John Blackburn

b.

c.

a.

b.

a.

Meneba Meel:

Flour Bags

Design Group

Millford-Van den Berg Design,
Wassenaar

Client

Meneba Meel

Designer

Erik de Graaf

Illustrator

Jeremy Sancha/Clare Mellinsky

Account Supervisor

Daphne Garschagen

b.

Van Den Bergh Foods:

Calve Meat and Fish Sauces

Design Group

Keja Donia Design, Amsterdam

Client

Van den Bergh Foods

Designer

Leon Bosboom/Willem Kroon

Photographer

Frans van Wijk

Illustrator

Hans Reizinger

Account Supervisor

Lex Donia

a.

b.

c.

d.

a,b.
Eurobest Award Winner
Koh-I-Noor:
Brushes and Combs
Design Group
Maurizio di Robilant &
Associates, Milan
Client
Koh-I-Noor
Designer
Maurizio di Robilant/
Lucia Sommaruga
Illustrator
Franco Sodano

c.
MCA:
Launch Promo Pack
Design Group
McCann-Erickson Manchester
Client
MCA
Designer
Dorina D'Ambrosio/Jason Edwards/
Glyn Wakefield
Creative Director
Keith Ravenscroft
Copywriter
Bryce Main
Illustrator
Dorina D'Ambrosio/Jason Edwards
Account Supervisor
Simon Clinton

d.
Vinsmoselle:
Art & Vin Limited Edition
Design Group
Made By Sams, Luxembourg
Client
Vinsmoselle
Designer
Carlos Moreira
Photographer
R.O.M. Studios/Raymond Clement
Account Supervisor
Will Kreutz

a.

Packaging and Design
Miscellaneous
p.110/111

a.
The Boots Company:
Boots Laundry Range
Design Group
Lewis Moberly, London
Client
The Boots Company
Designer
Kasia Rust/Mary Lewis

b.

b.
Goupil:
Fluokids Toothpastes and
Toothbrushes
Design Group
Raison Pure, Paris
Client
Goupil
Account Supervisor
Frédèric Jentgen

a.

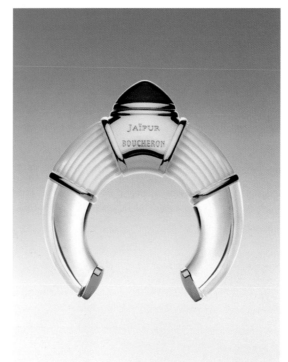

b.

c.

a,b,c.
Boucheron:
Jaïpur Perfumes
Design Group
Desgrippes & Associes, Paris
Client
Boucheron
Creative Director
Joël Desgrippes/Sophie Farhi
Account Supervisor
Marie-Hélène Prevot

d.
Swarovski:
The Designer's Scribble Book
Design Group
**Swarovski Communications,
Wattens**
Client
Swarovski Jewellery Stones
Designer
Stefan Rosentreter
Photographer
Michael Frank/Franz Eliskases
Account Supervisor
Theresia Adler-Kern

The Designer's Scribble Book From Swarovski Jewellery Stones

2

Herbst/Winter 93/94

Kleider
Manufaktur

HABSBURG

Feine Jagd- und
Gesellschaftskleidung

b.

a.

Kleidermanufaktur:

Fine Hunting & Society Fashion

Design Group

Demner & Merlicek, Vienna

Client

Kleidermanufaktur Habsburg

Designer

Franz Merlicek

Photographer

Bernhard Angerer

Illustrator

Jurgen Mick/Judith Modl

Account Supervisor

Annelies Litschauer

b.

John Partridge:

Corporate And Brand Identity

Design Group

Miller Sutherland, London

Client

John Partridge

Designer

Kathy Miller

Illustrator

Geoff Appleton

Account Supervisor

Sian Sutherland

Brewed Over Eire. Not Over 'Ere.
In judging the creative work of other people to find the true Eurobests, one of the major problems is being fair to all entries. To achieve this one has to understand the motivation behind an ad and its background and origin.
>A fine example of extraordinary local advertising is the outdoor poster for Beamish Stout, the Eurobest on page 118.
>It is evident proof of the fact that there are ads and campaigns which only a minority of Europeans can understand. And you will agree that language is the easiest barrier to overcome because it just has to be translated.
>But what about style, cultural background, political situation, just to name a few? Often, they cannot be explained — let alone be easily understood.
>The more European campaigns we see and the better we are aware of their advantages the more we also realize their limits. And thus we discover the power of local creativity.
>Judging is demanding and often means asking for an explanation from fellow jurors with different backgrounds. Because it must not happen that mediocre creative work — so called 'only-understood-by-creatives' — triumphs over brilliant stuff with a local background but a socio-geographically limited range of comprehensibility.
>Only with the will to discover can we realize that foreign ads are often better than ads brewed over 'ere.
Richard Schweizer, Lintas Zürich

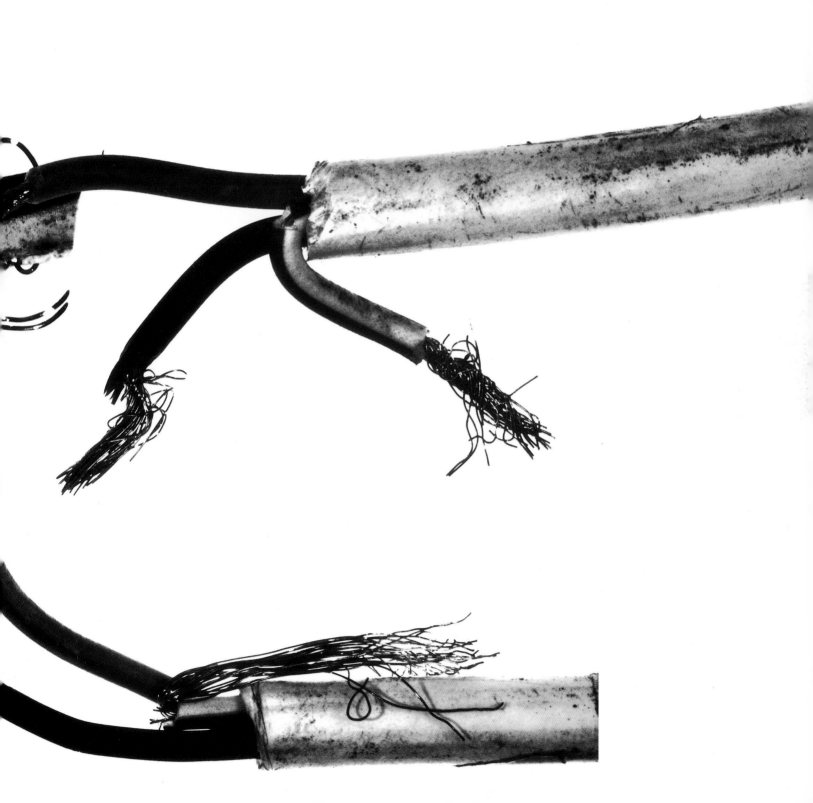

a.

b.

Strong teeth
Sugarfree
Stimorol

STIMOROL *free* ORIGINAL *With* XYLITOL

a.

Eurobest Award Winner
Gargoyles
Advertising Agency
Lowe Howard-Spink, London
Client
IDV
Creative Director
Paul Weinberger
Copywriter
Paul Falla
Art Director
Brian Campbell
Photographer
Mike Parsons
Account Supervisor
Liz Kelly
Advertiser's Supervisor
Paul Davey

b.

Eurobest Award Winner
Eire
Advertising Agency
Young & Rubicam, London
Client
Courage
Creative Director
Mike Cozens
Copywriter
Mike Cozens/Dave Henderson
Art Director
Sam Hurford
Photographer
Paul Murphy
Account Supervisor
Chris Hunton
Advertiser's Supervisor
Jerry Goldberg

c.

c.

Strong Teeth:
Lion
Advertising Agency
Aaseby Annonsbyrå, Helsingborg
Client
Stimorol
Copywriter
Björn Ståhl
Art Director
Johan Adelståhl
Account Supervisor
Gunilla Cox
Advertiser's Supervisor
Mattias Libell

a.

Outdoor

Food/ Household, Maintenance
and Pet Products

p.120/121

b.

c.

a.
There are climbers who shop
elsewhere — but they are getting
fewer.

a.
Falling Down
Advertising Agency
New Deal DDB Needham, Oslo
Client
Scandinavian Climbing Equipment
Copywriter
Steinar Borge
Art Director
Rune Markhus
Account Supervisor
Rune Roalsvig
Advertiser's Supervisor
Gunnar Østgaard

b.
Holes
Advertising Agency
BMP DDB Needham, London
Client
Schweppes
Creative Director
Tony Cox
Copywriter
Jeremy Craigen
Art Director
Jeremy Carr
Photographer
Mike Parsons
Account Supervisor
Simon Vessey

c.
Long Arms
Advertising Agency
BMP DDB Needham, London
Client
Schweppes
Creative Director
Tony Cox
Copywriter
Jeremy Craigen
Art Director
Jeremy Carr
Photographer
Amiel Pritsch
Account Supervisor
Simon Vessey

b.

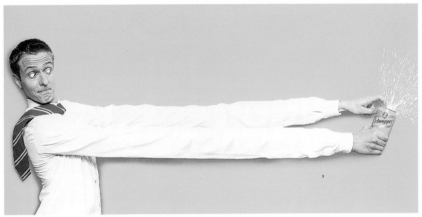

c.

d.

Language
Advertising Agency
Bartle Bogle Hegarty, London
Client
Coca-Cola
Creative Director
John Hegarty
Copywriter
Paul Silburn
Art Director
Tiger Savage
Illustrator
Mick Brownfield
Account Supervisor
Cindy Gallop
Advertiser's Supervisor
David Wheldon

d.

Kolbert in India ruit 249,–

c.
Jacket in Indian check 249,-

Kolbert in India geel 249,–

a.
Jacket in Indian yellow 249,-

Polo met Afrikaanse print 45,–

b.
Sports shirt with African print 45,-

a,b,c.
Eurobest Campaign Award Winner
Yellow Jacket
African Lady:Red
Checked Jacket
Advertising Agency
Campaign Company, Amsterdam
Client
Golden Town
Art Director
Béla Stamenkovits
Photographer
Hans Kroeskamp
Account Supervisor
Evaline Kruijssen
Advertiser's Supervisor
A.P. Boon

Outdoor
Colothing, Footwear and
Accessories
p.124/125

RALENTIR
ECOLE

PLANET
REEBOK

Reebok

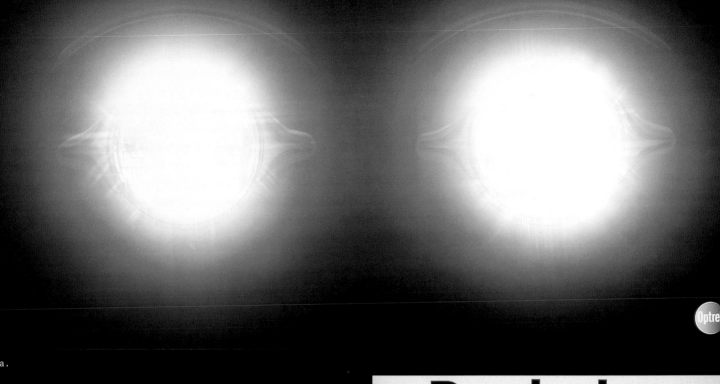

Bachelor.
New Golf GTD.

Married.
New Golf Variant.

Divorced.
New Golf Cabrio.

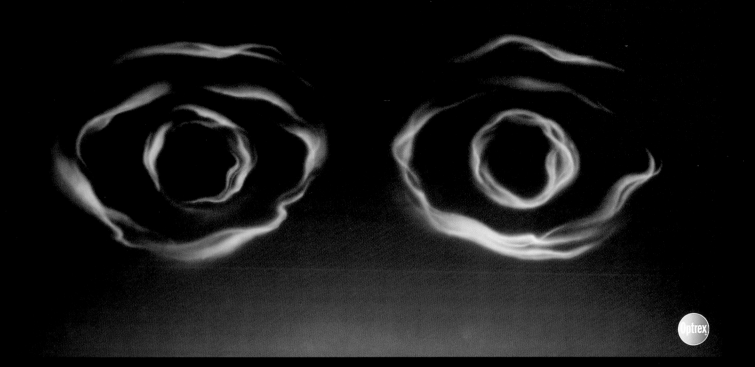

b.

POWER IS NOTHING WITHOUT CONTROL.

Carl Lewis is a member of the Santa Monica Track Club

IF YOU'RE GOING TO DRIVE, DRIVE **PIRELLI**

a.

a.
Carl Lewis
Advertising Agency
Young & Rubicam, London
Client
Pirelli
Creative Director
Mike Cozens
Copywriter
Ewan Paterson
Art Director
Graeme Norways
Photographer
Annie Leibovitz
Account Supervisor
David Gray/Emma Brock
Advertiser's Supervisor
Giancarlo Rocco

b,c,d.
Snow
River
Track
Advertising Agency
Bates Dorland, London
Client
Land Rover
Creative Director
Loz Simpson/Gerard Stamp
Copywriter
Loz Simpson
Art Director
Gerard Stamp
Photographer
Max Forsythe
Account Supervisor
Philip Lancaster
Advertiser's Supervisor
Russell Turnham

b.

c.

d.

a.
7 coats on every Mercedes.

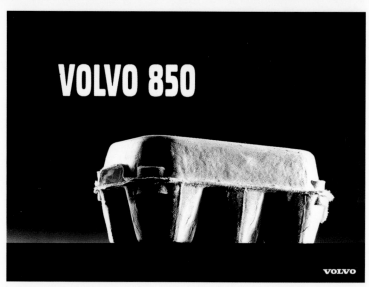

b.

Outdoor
Automotive/
Home Appliances, Furniture,
Audio-Visual and Home
Electronics/
Non-Commercial Public Services
and Charities
p.130/131

c.

d.
Photograph this poster, if you get
only one red colour, switch to a
new film.

e.
Deforestation rarely hits where
it hurts.

a.
4, 5, 6, 7 Coats
Advertising Agency
Campaign Company, Amsterdam
Client
**Mercedes-Benz Nederland/
Mediamax Buitenreclame**
Copywriter
Lysbeth Bijlstra
Art Director
Diederick Hillenius
Account Supervisor
Dik Klicks
Advertiser's Supervisor
Luc Schram

b.
Egg Carton
Advertising Agency
Forsman & Bodenfors, Gothenberg
Client
Volvo Personbilar Sverige
Copywriter
Filip Nilsson
Art Director
Mikko Timonen
Photographer
Fredrik Lieberath
Account Supervisor
Olle Victorin
Advertiser's Supervisor
**Anders Karlsson/
Olle Söderberg**

c,d.
Red
Advertising Agency
Young & Rubicam France, Boulogne
Client
Kodak Pathé
Creative Director
**Jean-Paul Bacquer/
Christian Vince**
Copywriter
Dominique Marchand
Art Director
Jean-Michel Alirol
Photographer
Richard Croft
Account Supervisor
Pauline Thureau Dangin
Advertiser's Supervisor
Philippe Veron

e.
Deforestation
Advertising Agency
Ogilvy & Mather Frankfurt
Client
WWF Frankfurt
Creative Director
Felix Glauner/Christoph Herold
Copywriter
Christoph Herold
Art Director
Felix Glauner
Account Supervisor
Sabine Frankl/Carola Romanus
Advertiser's Supervisor
Ulrike Hellmessen

a.

b.

a,b.

Eurobest Award Winner
Gotcha
Advertising Agency
BMP DDB Needham, London
Client
PowerBreaker
Creative Director
Tony Cox
Copywriter
Tony Davidson
Art Director
Tony Davidson
Typographer
Dave Wakefield
Account Supervisor
Ross Sleight/Mike Rayner

c.

Eurobest Award Winner
Phone
Advertising Agency
Saatchi & Saatchi, London
Client
Gallaher Tobacco
Creative Director
Alexandra Taylor
Copywriter
Jason Fretwell
Art Director
Nikolas Stuzinski
Photographer
Barney Edwards
Account Supervisor
Tim Duffy

d.

Director's Chair
Advertising Agency
Saatchi & Saatchi, London
Client
Gallaher Tobacco
Creative Director
Alexandra Taylor
Copywriter
John Messum/Paul Akins
Art Director
Alexandra Taylor
Photographer
Humberto Rivas
Account Supervisor
Moray MacLennan

7 mg TAR 0·7 mg NICOTINE
PROTECT CHILDREN: DON'T MAKE THEM BREATHE YOUR SMOKE
Health Departments' Chief Medical Officers

c.

7 mg TAR 0·7 mg NICOTINE
SMOKING CAUSES FATAL DISEASES
Health Departments' Chief Medical Officers

d.
Also a finalist in the
Photography Category

e.
Handbag
Advertising Agency
Saatchi & Saatchi, London
Client
Gallaher Tobacco
Creative Director
Alexandra Taylor
Copywriter
Eugene Ruane
Art Director
Casey Grady
Photographer
Satoshi Saikusa
Account Supervisor
Moray MacLennan

7 mg TAR 0·7 mg NICOTINE
SMOKING CAUSES CANCER
Health Departments' Chief Medical Officers

e.

a.

a.
Eurobest Award Winner
Car
Advertising Agency
TBWA Advertising, Amstelveen
Client
Toys R Us
Creative Director
Maarten Boog
Copywriter
Robert Oostinga/Maarten Boog
Art Director
Wil Oortgijs
Account Supervisor
Hans Kruijf/Eefje Moesbergen
Advertiser's Supervisor
Pim Bomas

London to New York. 7 times daily.

b.

Roken schaadt de gezondheid. Het kan longkanker of hartklachten veroorzaken. Kon. besluit van 29. 4. 1981, Stb. 329.

c.

b.
Graffiti Plane
Advertising Agency
Saatchi & Saatchi, London
Client
British Airways
Creative Director
James Lowther/Simon Dicketts
Copywriter
Richard Dean
Art Director
Martha Riley
Illustrator
Martha Riley
Account Supervisor
Tim Duffy
Advertiser's Supervisor
Derek Dear

c.
Nobody Makes Them...
Advertising Agency
FHV/BBDO, Amstelveen
Client
Douwe Egberts Van Nelle
Tabaksmaatschappij
Copywriter
Edward Bardoul
Art Director
Edward Bardoul/
Jan Paul Rey/Koeweiden Postma
Photographer
Yani

THE CHUBBIES – The fat people show – CHANNEL 1

a.

THE WALL STREET JOURNAL EUROPE.
* * *

NO PHOTOS

To get in the way
of the beautiful
graphs, statistics
and WORDS.

Read It.

The Simpsons.
You saw it first on Sky.

Sky News. On the hour, every hour, 24 hours.

NO TURNING BACK

c.

The F.A. Premiership. Exclusively live on Sky Sports.

Great news for divorce solicitors. Premier league football is back.

NO TURNING BACK

d.

Cause of death: Madonna.

Body of Evidence. Madonna — Willem Dafoe. The British TV Premiere, Saturday 17th September on Sky Movies.

NO TURNING BACK

e.

b.
No Photos
Advertising Agency
Wieden & Kennedy, Amsterdam
Client
Wall Street Journal Europe
Creative Director
Michael Prieve
Copywriter
Bob Moore
Art Director
Bernd Sanmann
Account Supervisor
Rachel Stewart/Regina van Hoof
Advertiser's Supervisor
Chris Fitzgerald

c.
Simpsons
Advertising Agency
Bartle Bogle Hegarty, London
Client
Sky TV
Creative Director
John Hegarty
Copywriter
John McCabe
Art Director
Tim Ashton
Account Supervisor
Gwyn Jones
Advertiser's Supervisor
Simon Morris

d.
Divorce
Advertising Agency
Bartle Bogle Hegarty, London
Client
Sky TV
Creative Director
John Hegarty
Copywriter
Paul Silburn
Art Director
Tiger Savage
Photographer
Kerry Wilson
Account Supervisor
Gwyn Jones
Advertiser's Supervisor
Simon Morris

e.
Body Of Evidence
Advertising Agency
Bartle Bogle Hegarty, London
Client
Sky TV
Creative Director
John Hegarty
Copywriter
Paul Silburn
Art Director
Tiger Savage
Illustrator
Mick Brownfield
Account Supervisor
Gwyn Jones
Advertiser's Supervisor
Simon Morris

a.

Du 18 au 31 octobre
52-60, av. des Champs-Elysées, Paris.

Virgin
MEGASTORE

ANNIVERSAIRE DU VIRGIN MEGASTORE.
TOUTE ABSENCE SERA SEVEREMENT PUNIE.

b.
Virgin Megastore Anniversary:
anyone missing it will be
severely punished.

Outdoor
Retail Stores, Retail Chains
and Restaurants
p.138/139

c.

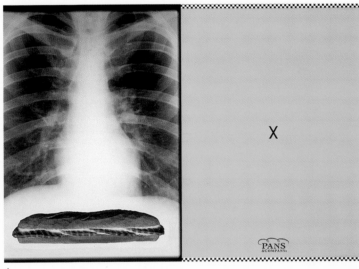

d.

a.
The Cat
Advertising Agency
TBWA, Brussels
Client
La Redoute
Creative Director
Andre Rysman
Art Director
Laurent Diercxsens
Photographer
Frank Uyttenhove
Account Supervisor
Bernadette Joos
Advertiser's Supervisor
François Senechal/
Veronique Vermeulen

b.
Anniversaire
Advertising Agency
BDDP, Boulogne
Client
Virgin Megastore
Creative Director
Marie-Catherine Dupuy/
Jean-Pierre Barbou
Copywriter
Rémi Babinet
Art Director
Philippe Pollet Villard
Photographer
Philippe Pollet Villard
Account Supervisor
Diane Attali
Advertiser's Supervisor
Jérôme Piot

c.
Hawaiian
Advertising Agency
Delvico Bates Barcelona
Client
Pans & Company
Creative Director
Félix Fernandez de Castro/
Toni Segarra
Copywriter
Gloria Hernández
Art Director
David Caballero
Account Supervisor
Javier Bernal

d.
X-Ray
Advertising Agency
Delvico Bates Barcelona
Client
Pans & Company
Creative Director
David Caballero/
Toni Segarra/
Félix Fernandez
de Castro
Copywriter
David Caballero
Art Director
David Caballero
Photographer
Marcus Welby
Account Supervisor
Javier Bernal

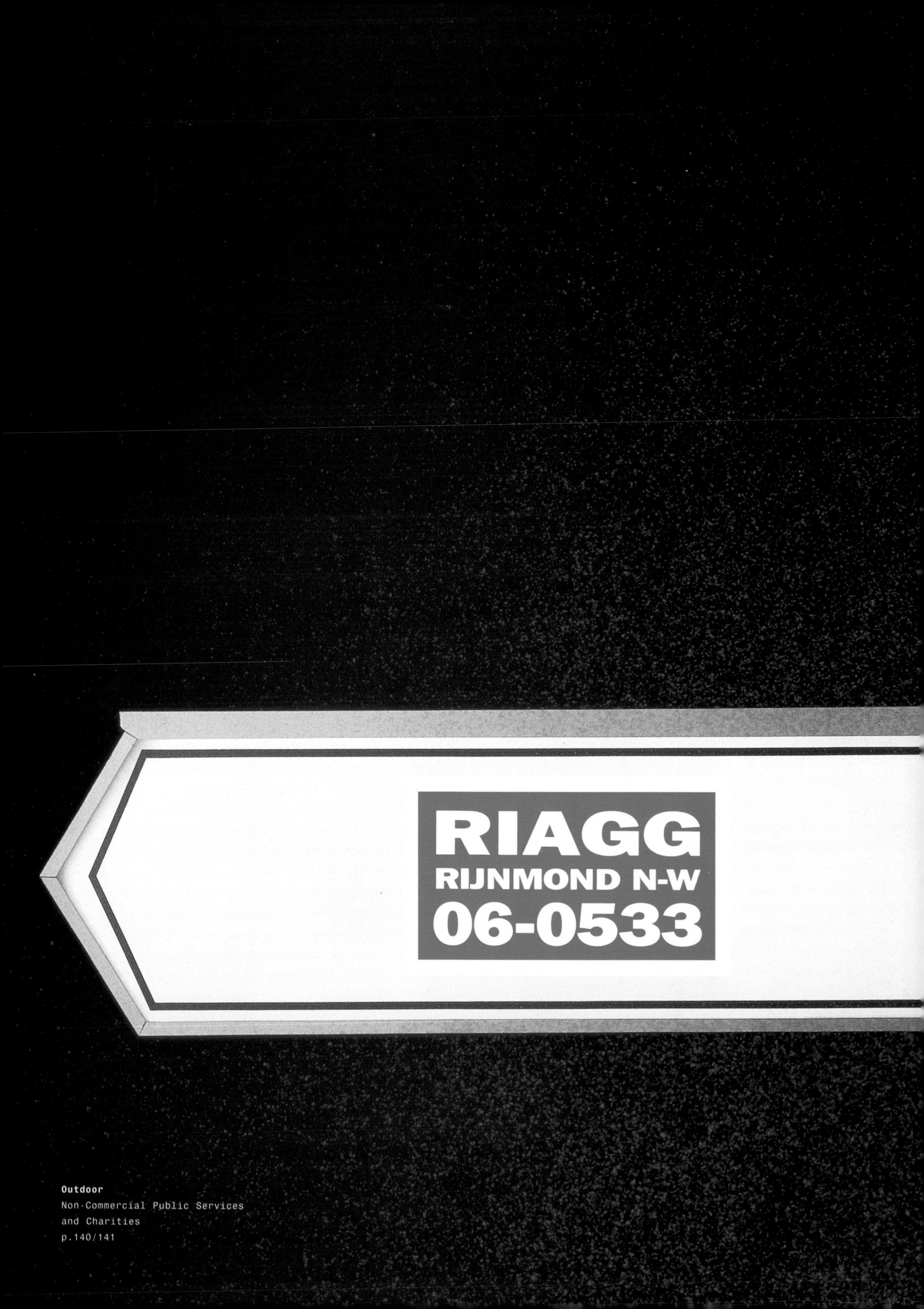
RIAGG
RIJNMOND N-W
06-0533

Outdoor
Non-Commercial Public Services
and Charities
p.140/141

Lourdes

Lourdes
Advertising Agency
Campaign Company, Amsterdam
Client
**Riagg Rijnmond Noord-West
(Psychiatric Help)**
Copywriter
Poppe van Pelt
Art Director
Thierry Somers
Photographer
Paul Ruigrok
Account Supervisor
Mechteld Snouck
Advertiser's Supervisor
J.F. Lamé

EUGENIO FABOZZI ONORANZE FUNEBRI ✆ 23 23 23 23

a.
How much of yourself do you send
up in smoke every day?
Eugenio Fabozzi Funeral Home.

EUGENIO FABOZZI ONORANZE FUNEBRI ✆ 23 23 23 23

b.
Vintage crack-up.
Eugenio Fabozzi Funeral Home.

a,b,c.
Quanto Sfumi Al Giorno?
Perché Arrivare Prima?
Schianti Classico
Advertising Agency
Reggio Del Bravo Pubblicita',
Rome
Client
Eugenio Fabozzi Onoranze
Funebri
Creative Director
Agostino Reggio/Paolo Del Bravo
Copywriter
Paolo Del Bravo
Art Director
Agostino Reggio
Illustrator
Daniele Melani
Account Supervisor
Paola Rota
Advertiser's Supervisor
Walter Fabozzi

d.
Two Breasts
Advertising Agency
Delvico Bates Barcelona
Client
Spanish Cancer Association
(AECC)
Creative Director
Toni Segarra/
Félix Fernandez de Castro
Copywriter
Pablo Monzón
Art Director
David Caballero
Photographer
Isabel Valls
Account Supervisor
Marta Turón

Outdoor
Commercial Public Services/
Non-Commercial Public Services
and Charities

PERCHE' ARRIVARE PRIMA?

SPIDER

EUGENIO FABOZZI ONORANZE FUNEBRI ☎ **23 23 23 23**

c.
Why rush to get there first?
Eugenio Fabozzi Funeral Home.

If you feel
ashamed
about show-
ing your
two breasts,
imagine
showing just
one.

CONTRA EL CANCER

d.

Did the Best Commercials Win in Eurobest 1994?

A jury will always be subject to a certain degree of disagreement, and each member will have to accept that some of his favourites don't qualify. >(Nike presented a unique film featuring football player Eric Cantona, which to my surprise wasn't even included on the shortlist.)

>Having said so, I still feel that this year's winners represent a dignified selection of the best productions of '94. >Some of the most exciting moments during the evaluation were seeing the commercials from Russia. Though the commercial industry in this country is still at an infancy stage, they have managed to establish an impressive level of quality. And considering the wisdom and elegance characterizing other artistic modes of expression in Russia, my prediction is that this country is soon to become one of the world's leading commercial contributors.

>Another, and not so pleasing development seems to be inspired by the music channel MTV with its domineering and repetitive visual language. In several productions the camera is being handled like a fire extinguisher, and the message edited into oblivion. >To quote feature film director Sidney Pollack's words of wisdom: "Any idiot can move the camera, but it takes a genius to move the audience."

Johan Gulbranson, Leo Film/ Leo Burnett Oslo

Dog

Advertising Agency
New Deal DDB Needham, Oslo
Client
Stabburet
Copywriter
Knut Georg Andresen
Art Director
Gro Norderval Gulbrandsen
Production Company
Big Deal, Oslo
Producer
Turid Øversveen
Director
Pål Sletaune

A man enters the kitchen heading for the freezer. He takes a package of A la Carte out of the freezer. He opens the package and puts the dish into the microwave oven.
"It takes only eight minutes to make an A la Carte meal."
"Meanwhile you can air the dog."
The man opens the kitchen window and holds the dog out of the window.
Delicious meals for busy people.

Refurnishing
Advertising Agency
New Deal DDB Needham, Oslo
Client
Stabburet
Copywriter
Knut Georg Andresen
Art Director
Gro Norderval Gulbrandsen
Production Company
Big Deal, Oslo
Producer
Turid Øversveen
Director
Pål Sletaune

A woman enters the kitchen heading for the freezer. She takes a package of A la Carte out of the freezer. She goes to the microwave oven, opens the package and puts the dish into the microwave oven.
"It takes only eight minutes to make an A la Carte meal."
"Meanwhile you can re-furnish the room."
The woman takes one of the two chairs around the table and moves it to the next free space. She does the same with the other chair too.
Delicious meals for busy people.

Eurobest Award Winner
Footballer
Advertising Agency
Advico Young & Rubicam, Zürich
Client
ZVSM — Milk
Creative Director
Hansjörg Zürcher
Copywriter
Matthias Freuler
Art Director
Erik Voser
Production Company
Voyager Film, London
Producer
Linda Peryer
Director
Bill Marshall

A soccer player and a cow. The
man does tricks with the ball,
prompts the cow to do likewise,
and realizes with resignation
that the cow out-tricks him.
>Gives you the kick.
Milk. The natural high.

"...I have done a great deal of
work on black holes, and all
would be wasted if it turns

"...I have done a great deal of
work on black holes, and all
would be wasted if it turns out
black holes do not exist..."

A Brief History of Time
-Stephen W. Hawking-

Don't

worry

Stephen.

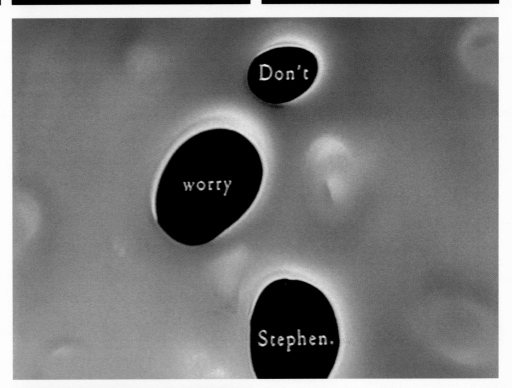

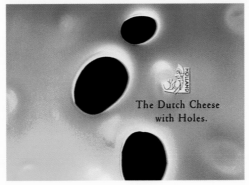

Holes
Advertising Agency
Delvico Bates Barcelona
Client
Cheeses from Holland
Creative Director
Toni Segarra/
Félix Fernandez de Castro
Copywriter
Toni Segarra
Art Director
David Caballero
Agency Producer
David Caballero
Production Company
Ricardo Albiñana Films,
Barcelona
Producer
Ricardo Albiñana
Director
Ricardo Albiñana

"...I have done a great deal of
work on black holes, and all
would be wasted if it turns out
black holes do not exist..."
A Brief History of Time —
Stephen Hawking.
>Black screen. The words "Don't
worry Stephen" appear one after
the other. Then holes begin to
appear in the cheese.
The Dutch cheese with holes.

La Pasta Della Passione
Advertising Agency
**Paradiset DDB Needham,
Stockholm**
Client
Kungsörnen
Creative Director
Paul Malmström/Linus Karlsson
Copywriter
Linus Karlsson
Art Director
Paul Malmström
Production Company
Moland Film, Stockholm
Director
Marius Holst
Music
Housework

A lunch drama somewhere in
southern Europe where a simple
bowl of Turelli spaghetti turns
a young couple on and revives
the passion of an elderly couple
at a table nearby.

Television and Cinema
Savoury Foods
p.150/151

Restaurant

Advertising Agency
BSB Bates Benjamin, Oslo
Client
Tine Norwegian Dairy
Copywriter
Dagmar Kollstrøm
Art Director
Carl-Erik Conforto
Production Company
Bates Film, Oslo
Producer
Lis Pedersen
Director
Pål Sletaune
Lighting Cameraman
Peder Norlund

We are in the kitchen of a fine restaurant. A young waiter gazes into the restaurant with an expression of amazement. He turns towards the cook:
"Did you have anything special in that sauce?"
"A dash of cream, how come?"
"I was just wondering..."
The waiter looks into the restaurant again. We cut to the guests who are enthusiastically licking their plates.
Tine Cream Enhances the Taste.

Soup Station
Advertising Agency
BSB Bates Benjamin, Oslo
Client
Tine Norwegian Dairy
Copywriter
Dagmar Kollstrøm
Art Director
Carl-Erik Conforto
Production Company
Bates Film, Oslo
Producer
Lis Pedersen
Director
Pål Sletaune
Lighting Cameraman
Peder Norlund

We see a soup station in the middle of the Norwegian countryside. All the competitors are enjoying the soup. There is a cheerful atmosphere. The soup tastes so good that nobody wants to leave the soup station to continue the race. We cut to the finishing-line. It is abandoned except for two officials, who continue to wait for the competitors to arrive.
Tine Cream Enhances the Taste.

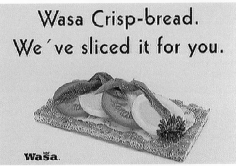

Easter Wasa
Advertising Agency
JBR Reklamebyrå, Oslo
Client
Ideal Wasa
Creative Director
Kjetil Try
Copywriter
Kjetil Try
Art Director
Einar Fjøsne
Production Company
JBR Film, Oslo
Producer
Torleif Hauge
Director
Erik Poppe
Lighting Cameraman
Erik Poppe
Music
Wim Mertens

It is Easter in the mountains.
We see various comic situations
where people struggle to slice
a loaf of stale bread.
**Wasa Crisp-bread. We've sliced
it for you.**

Camping-Wasa

Wasa
Lett å feriere med

Camping Wasa
Advertising Agency
JBR Reklamebyrå, Oslo
Client
Ideal Wasa
Creative Director
Kjetil Try
Copywriter
Kjetil Try
Art Director
Einar Fjøsne
Production Company
JBR Film, Oslo
Producer
Torleif Hauge
Director
Erik Poppe
Lighting Cameraman
Erik Poppe
Music
Wim Mertens

We are at a campsite and it is raining very heavily. Several campers are trying to light their barbecues without success. This commercial shows various comic situations where people desperately try to light their barbecues.
Camping-Wasa

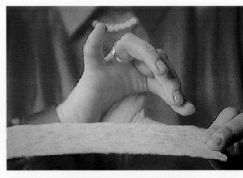

Eurobest Award Winner
Ideal Wasa
Advertising Agency
JBR Reklamebyrå, Oslo
Client
Ideal Wasa
Creative Director
Kjetil Try
Copywriter
Kjetil Try
Art Director
Einar Fjøsne
Production Company
JBR Film, Oslo
Producer
Torleif Hauge
Director
Kjetil Try
Lighting Cameraman
Svein Krøvel

Kate, a booking assistant, is being interviewed about new Ideal Home-made Wasa crispbread. "So, I think it's just great." "I'd never expected it to be this thin and at the same time so easy to spread. I feel much more secure, it doesn't break, it doesn't crunch."
A voice-over informs us that: "Whereas other brands break, Ideal Home-made has a unique spreading ability which prevents breaking."
"Ideal Home-made — like home-made should be!"
"I'm just extremely satisfied with it, and the only thing I can say is; if you haven't tried it yet — try it."
Ideal Home-made.

NO NUTS NO GLORY

Eurobest Campaign Award Winner
Lightbulb
Waste Disposal Bag
Advertising Agency
Lintas Amsterdam
Client

We see a boy in a garage. In one
hand he holds a Nuts candybar,
in the other a garbage bag. He
takes a bite from his Nuts bar.
In his eyes you can see that
there is something about to
happen. The garage door swings
open and he walks to the side-
walk with the garbage bag in his
hand. The music becomes louder
and the boy puts the garbage bag

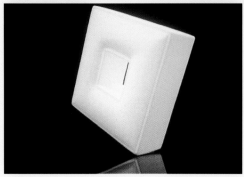

Eurobest Campaign Award Winner
Ruota
Foglia
Advertising Agency
J Walter Thompson Italia, Milan
Client
Nestlé Italiana
Copywriter
Enrico Chiarugi
Art Director
Luca Maroni
Production Company
BRW & Partners, Milan
Producer
Daniela Cattaneo
Director
Alberto Zabban/Luca Maroni
Lighting Cameraman
Alberto Zabban

"Long is the road that leads to perfection!"
At long last, after the triangle wheel, the square wheel, the round wheel, mankind has invented the mint wheel.
"And it is full of holes."
Polo, the mint with the hole.

IL BUCO CON LA MENTA INTORNO

POLO

"Polo, the mint reserved for
adults only is now available to
under eighteens."
Polo, the mint with the hole.

SOME ADVICE TO THE WORLD'S STOCK MARKETS

FROM THE MASTER PATISSIERS OF DELACRE

CALM DOWN   IF WE MADE BISCUITS THE WAY YOU DO BUSINESS

 WE'D HAVE DISASTERS IN THE KITCHEN TOO

 GREAT BISCUITS

Tell your broker

The frenetic workings of the world's stockmarkets are contrasted with the careful and thoughtful methods followed in their atelier by the master patissiers of Delacre.

Stock Market
Advertising Agency
Ogilvy & Mather, Paris
Client
Delacre
Creative Director
Bernard Bureau
Copywriter
Steve Jeffery
Art Director
Steve Jeffery
Agency Producer
Evelyne Callot
Production Company
RSA Films, London
Editor
Marc Alchin
Music
"William Tell Overture":
Rossini

Television and Cinema
Sweet Foods and Confectionery/
Alcoholic Drinks
p.162/163

"Some advice to the world's stockmarkets."
"From the master patissiers of Delacre."
"Calm down."
"Take it easy."
"Relax."
"That's the way we make biscuits."
"And they always turn out wonderful."
"If we made biscuits the way you do business..."
"...I'm quite sure..."
"...We'd have disasters in the kitchen too."
"The master patissiers of Delacre make great biscuits."
"Tell your broker."
Delacre. Great Biscuits.

Steady Can
Advertising Agency
Bartle Bogle Hegarty, London
Client
The Whitbread Beer Company
Creative Director
John Hegarty
Copywriter
John McCabe
Art Director
Tim Ashton
Agency Producer
Rebecca Atkinson
Production Company
RSA Films, London
Producer
Adrian Harrison
Director
John Marles
Lighting Cameraman
Brian Bronsgrove

This commercial resembles a TV variety show in Sydney, Australia. It's called Channel Tooheys.
"Put your hands together and welcome Mr Milt Bailey."
"Hi Milt."
"Now, Milt you invented the steady can?"
"Er, no steady cam, as in steady camera."
"Not as in can?"
"Er, no...no."
"Well, what point is there in steadying a camera?"
"Yeah, it's not like anything's going to spill out of it if you knock it over, is it?"
"No, well, when you're..."
"Absolutely. Unfortunately, we've just about run out of time on the show today. Milt if you need a cab or anything, camera 3 will sort it out."
Tooheys Export. Brewed in Sydney since 1869.

This commercial is a parody of a glamorous sun cream commercial shot on an idyllic beach.
>Music — 'Stay Just a Little Bit Longer'.
>A montage of beautiful women and muscled men in swimwear.
"Now there's a cream that helps you stay in the sun just a little bit longer."
The camera pans across the face of a beautiful girl. She brings a pint of Boddingtons up to her lips.
"By 'eck, I could stay here as long as you like chuck."
Her boyfriend looks like a film star, silhouetted against a pure blue sky. The blue however, is the side of a blue lorry. It pulls away to reveal Blackpool tower and illuminations.
"'Ere Vera, fancy a top up, luv? ...eh?"
"Not 'alf, and give us another rub down with that chip fat."
A small plane flies across the sky towing a banner:
Boddingtons.
The Cream of Manchester.

Television and Cinema
Alcoholic Drinks
p.164/165

Bavaria Night
Advertising Agency
Forsman & Bodenfors, Gothenburg
Client
Falcon
Copywriter
Filip Nilsson
Art Director
Mark Whitehouse
Production Company
Studio 24, Stockholm
Producer
Per Arte
Director
Roy Andersson
Lighting Cameraman
Istvan Borbas
Music
Stockholms Mässingsseptett

Music — Loud Bavarian Brass Music
>A middle-aged couple are having dinner in their drab little kitchen, but the loud Bavarian music from a party next door, which is shaking their kitchen interior, annoys them. The husband decides to do something about it and gets out of his chair.
"That's enough."
His wife agrees.
>He goes next door to complain, while his wife waits at the dinner table. Finally he ends up joining what has turned out to be a very jolly Bavarian night.
**Falcon Bayerskt Class I.
It's Bavaria at home.**

Television and Cinema
Alcoholic Drinks
p.166/167

Storytellers
Advertising Agency
Saatchi & Saatchi, London
Client
Carlsberg-Tetley Brewing
Creative Director
James Lowther/Simon Dicketts
Copywriter
John Pallant
Art Director
Matt Ryan
Agency Producer
Vic Saunders
Production Company
Limelight, London
Producer
Caroline Warner
Director
John Lloyd
Lighting Cameraman
John Seale
Music
Paul Hart/Jo Campbell

A farmer's daughter skips
through the Australian outback.
"Hello sky, hello birds, hello
sheep", she cries, "isn't it a
beautiful day."
>She comes across a pool
surrounded by trees, where a
frog is sitting.
"Hello, Mr Frog", she says,
"I'll bet if I was to kiss you,
I bet you'd turn into a
handsome sheep shearer."
She blows the frog a kiss and in
a magical puff of smoke, the
frog turns into a handsome sheep
shearer. She puckers her lips to
be kissed and when she is, to
the sheep shearer's delight, she
turns into a glass of
Castlemaine XXXX lager.
>He sips the beer and a voice-
over says: "Castlemaine is made
with golden cluster hops."
He then whispers to the can,
"you haven't got any sisters,
have you?"
**"Experienced hoppers wouldn't
give a XXXX for anything else".**

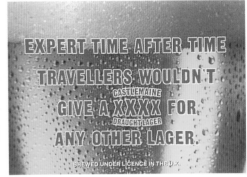

Eurobest Award Winner
Time Travellers
Advertising Agency
Saatchi & Saatchi, London
Client
Carlsberg-Tetley Brewing
Creative Director
James Lowther/Simon Dicketts
Copywriter
Dave Fowle
Art Director
Keith Terry
Agency Producer
Vic Saunders
Production Company
Limelight, London
Producer
Caroline Warner
Director
John Lloyd
Lighting Cameraman
John Seale
Music
Paul Hart/Jo Campbell

Open on a secret installation miles from anywhere.
>Inside the laboratory an excited looking scientist springs to life.
"You've done it professor!"
"Yep."
"You've invented the time machine!"
"Yep."
The professor opens a can of XXXX and pours it into a glass.
"You can witness the dawn of creation!"
"Yep."
"See real live dinosaurs!"
"Yep."
"Witness Captain Cook's first step onto the golden shores of Australia."
"Yep."
Whilst the assistant jabbers on, the professor drinks his XXXX. He finishes the can and presses a button on the time machine.
"You've done it professor."
The sequence repeats itself.
>As the assistant jabbers on, the professor enjoys his refilled can of XXXX for a second time. The professor finishes his can and presses a button on the time machine.
>The sequence starts again, but this time a stream of light catches the professors new pint of XXXX.
"Castlemaine is made from golden cluster hops..."
"This could go on forever."
He takes a swig of lager.
"Expert time after time travellers wouldn't give a Castlemaine XXXX for any other lager".

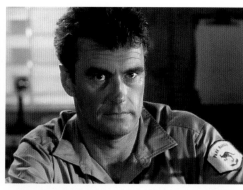

Behind Bars
Advertising Agency
Saatchi & Saatchi, London
Client
Carlsberg-Tetley Brewing
Creative Director
James Lowther/Simon Dicketts
Copywriter
Neil Pavitt
Art Director
Colin Jones
Agency Producer
Vic Saunders
Production Company
Limelight, London
Producer
Caroline Warner
Director
John Lloyd
Lighting Cameraman
John Seale
Music
Paul Hart/Jo Campbell

We open on a tiny jail in the outback.
>We cut to inside where we see a man who has been caught poaching, having his personal belongings logged in by two park rangers.
>The first ranger names each item and the second repeats it as he writes it down.
>The poacher then puts two cans of Castlemaine on the table.
"Two cans of Castlemaine" says the first ranger.
>The second ranger remains silent. The poacher, realising he's not going to get his Castlemaine back, slams his watch down on the table.
"One watch, broken", says the first ranger.
"One watch, broken", says the second.
>We cut to the two rangers sitting outside the pub both drinking glasses of Castlemaine.
>From inside the jail we hear the poacher shout, "you guys wouldn't be using my comb out there would you?"
"Nope" says the first.
"Nope" says the second.
"Experts behind bars wouldn't give a XXXX for anything else."

Eurobest Award Winner
Credibility
Advertising Agency
BMP DDB Needham, London
Client
Courage
Creative Director
Tony Cox
Copywriter
John Webster/Jack Dee
Art Director
John Webster
Agency Producer
Lucinda Ker
Production Company
Fletcher Sanderson Films/
Open Mike Productions, London
Producer
Madeleine Sanderson/
David Morley
Director
Mandie Fletcher
Lighting Cameraman
Richard Greatrex
Music
Vince Pope

Jack Dee in an armchair talks about a new can of John Smith's Draught in his hand.
"After 100 years you can now enjoy John Smith's Draught in a can. It's got a widget for that just served by the landlord taste, so...I'm not doing this."
>The Director interrupts:
"Don't you like the beer?"
Jack retorts:
"I like the beer — it's just not my material — it's degrading."
He picks up a vase of flowers from the table and indicates the script stuck to the back.
>The Director argues but Jack is adamant.
"I'm sorry, I'm not prepared to compromise my hard man of comedy image — I mean why should I?"
A bag of money is thrown onto the table. Suddenly dancing girls dressed as ladybirds appear.
>The girls and Jack sing:
"Widget, it's got a widget, a lovely widget, a widget it has got..." (fade).
>Cut to can:
John Smith's Draught Bitter.
No nonsense.

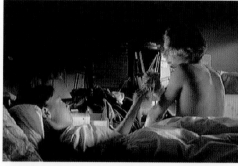

Solo Condom
Advertising Agency
JBR Reklamebyrå, Oslo
Client
Solo
Creative Director
Kjetil Try
Copywriter
Frode Karlberg
Art Director
Bjørn Smørholm
Production Company
JBR Film, Oslo
Producer
Torleif Hauge
Director
Pål Sletaune
Lighting Cameraman
Jon Kristian Rosenlund
Music
Geir Bøhn/Bent Aaserud

A teenage couple are in bed.
The young man struggles with a
condom but is unable to put it
on properly. A sip of his soft
drink doesn't help. Eventually
the girl falls asleep.
**Solo. Probably the only soft
drink that helps nothing but
thirst.**

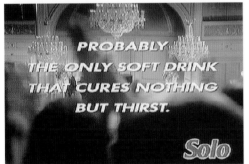

Solo Opera
Advertising Agency
JBR Reklamebyrå, Oslo
Client
Solo
Creative Director
Kjetil Try
Copywriter
Frode Karlberg
Art Director
Bjørn Smørholm
Production Company
JBR Film, Oslo
Producer
Torleif Hauge
Director
Pål Sletaune
Lighting Cameraman
Jon Kristian Rosenlund

Olga Marie Mikalsen is an eccentric performer who is singing 'Happy Birthday' out of tune. She takes a sip of her soft drink but still continues to sing out of tune. **Solo. Probably the only soft drink that helps nothing but thirst.**

Goliath

Advertising Agency
Bartle Bogle Hegarty, London

Client
A.G. Barr

Creative Director
John Hegarty

Copywriter
Tim Riley

Art Director
Mike Wells

Agency Producer
Geoff Stickler

Production Company
Park Village Productions, London

Producer
Kirstie McLeod

Director
Peter Webb

Lighting Cameraman
Ian McMillan

Two armies face each other
across the desert.
"And so, our two greatest
warriors must do battle..."
"David..."
"...and Goliath."
"Look little guy, there's no
need to fight over this. Let's
talk it through over a can of
Irn Bru."
"Another bleeding heart
liberal...save it, thunder
thighs!"
"But violence never solved
anything."
"Just my luck. An eight foot boy
scout. You heard the man. Let''s
go!"
David hurls a stone in Goliath's
direction.
Cut to Goliath. He's now wearing
a modern motorcycle helmet. The
stone ricochets off it
harmlessly.
"Well, who says the film has to
be like the book?"
David gulps and turns to run, as
a giant shadow falls over him.
Think Different.
Drink Different. Irn Bru.

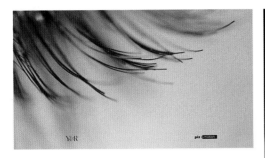

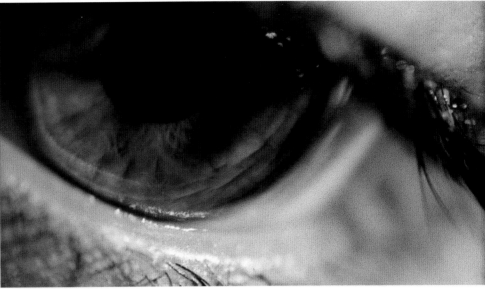

Is dit straks het enige natuurlijke water dat ons rest?

The Tear
Advertising Agency
Young & Rubicam, Brussels
Client
Spadel
Creative Director
Guillaume van der Stighelen
Copywriter
Willem de Geyndt
Art Director
Dominique van Doormaal
Agency Producer
Bernard Cornut
Production Company
Pix & Motion, Brussels
Producer
Anemie Maes
Director
Stef Viaene

Melancholy gypsy-like music.
>Close-up of an eye. The eyelid
moves a few times. All of a
sudden water wells up in it.
And a tear falls down. Text
appears at the same time:
"One day, will this be the only
natural water left to us?"
"When Man cares for Water, Water
cares for Man."

Spa.

 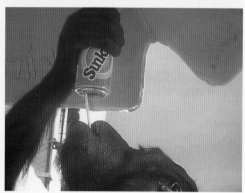 

Orangeetang
Advertising Agency
Saatchi & Saatchi, London
Client
Schweppes GB
Creative Director
James Lowther/Simon Dicketts
Copywriter
Adam Kean/Jason Fretwell
Art Director
Alexandra Taylor/Nik Studzinski
Agency Producer
Jim Baker
Production Company
Paul Weiland Film Company, London
Producer
Paul Rothwell
Director
Mike Stephenson
Lighting Cameraman
Barry Brown
Music
Joe & Co.

Television and Cinema
Non-Alcoholic Drinks/
Household, Maintenance Products
and Pet Products
p.174/175

An orang-utan travels to L.A. and hitches a ride into town. We hear his thoughts as he mouths off about the lifestyle.
"Why did I come to a lunatic asylum like California?"
He cruises past jogging babes.
"For the women? I don't think so, bodies too long, arms too short. Get out of here!"
He sees women having treatment in a beauty parlour.
"Why? To get a face lift? 5,000 miles for a tummy tuck, buttock suck, all over pluck, not me pal! Collagen injections? With my lips?"
He shares a jacuzzi with a Hollywood producer.
"A word of advice Mr L.A., never eat a chilli before you take a bath."
He watches a woman puffing and panting on an exercise bike.
"Hey! What's the matter lady? Someone stolen your wheels?"
He heads up into the hills to drink Sunkist.
"Why California? Sunkist is why. You want real taste, you gotta have real oranges, okay. So this place got one thing right."
Cut to later. He is being carried off by a couple of policemen.
"Hey! You guys got something against long hair, or what?"
Sunkist.

Wij van WC-EEND adviseren WC-EEND.

Parfum
Advertising Agency
Lowe Kuiper & Schouten,
Amsterdam
Client
WC-Eend
Creative Director
Bart Kuiper
Copywriter
Hans van Dijk
Art Director
Bart Kuiper
Agency Producer
Sandra Hendriksen
Production Company
Will van der Vlugt Film
Productions, Amsterdam
Producer
Marlies van Heese
Director
Bart Kuiper
Lighting Cameraman
Ronald Koetzier

We see a perfume bottle rotating.
"From the Geilefeld house comes
Sensuela, a naughty perfume."
Dissolve to another rotating
perfume bottle:
"And from the Sashimi house
comes Yaki...not bad either."
Dissolve to the WC-Duck product
on a rotating toilet seat.
"But the biggest sensation comes
from the house WC-Duck. With
Potpourri, a bouquet of freshness
for every shithouse."
"And that's why we from WC-Duck
recommend...WC-Duck."

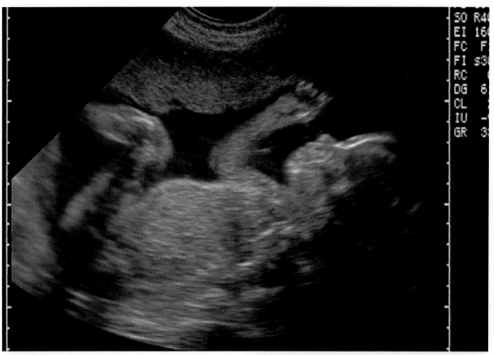

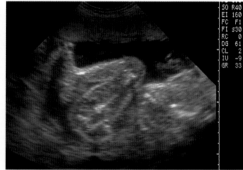

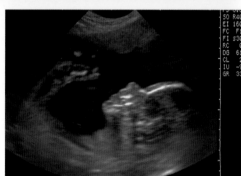

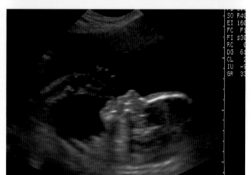

WHEN MAN CARES FOR WATER,
WATER CARES FOR MAN.

The Echography
Advertising Agency
Young & Rubicam, Brussels
Client
Spadel
Creative Director
Guillaume van der Stighelen
Copywriter
Thierry de Caluwe
Art Director
Stephanie Berryer
Agency Producer
Bernard Cornut
Production Company
Banana Split, Brussels
Producer
Jean-Luc Van Damme
Director
Serge Honorez

We see an echography of a foetus
in the womb. The baby moves very
slowly each time he hiccups.
>A glass of water appears on the
screen indicating that the
mother is drinking Spa.
>The hiccups stop and the baby
puts his thumb in his mouth.
"When Man cares for Water, Water
cares for Man."
Spa.

Tourtel 100%
Advertising Agency
BDDP, Boulogne
Client
Kanterbrau
Creative Director
Marie-Catherine Dupuy/
Jean-Pierre Barbou
Copywriter
Olivier Altman
Art Director
Robin de Lestrade
Agency Producer
Frédéric Blamont
Production Company
Telema, Levallois-Perret
Producer
Charles Gassot
Director
Régis Ceyrac

A man is paid by his boss. 3% honest. He jumps into his car and rips his shirt. 40% synthetic. He drives past a stray dog. 25% bulldog. He runs out of petrol. 0% gas. He enters a bar and walks past a pretty girl. 50% blonde. He orders a drink.
100% pure malt. Tourtel.
100% pure malt. 0% compromise.

Eurobest Award Winner
Restaurant
Advertising Agency
Lintas Amsterdam
Client
Nestlé Nederland
Creative Director
Jan Van Meel
Copywriter
Diederick Koopal
Art Director
Joep de Kort
Agency Producer
Cariola van Beek
Production Company
**René van den Bergh Produkties,
Amsterdam**
Producer
René van den Bergh
Director
Diederick Koopal/Joep de Kort
Lighting Cameraman
Michael Steenmeijer
Music
Wim Vonk/Marcel Walvisch

A cat sits behind the door of a
'restaurant' receiving cat
guests. In the background we can
hear lovely restaurant music.
Cats from different environments
enter the restaurant through the
hatch. Everything goes according
to plan. Until...a dachshund
puts its head through the hatch.
The cat gives him what for. The
dachshund's head disappears with
a loud howl.
>We see a shot of the restaurant.
Cats dine with Gourmet.

Television and Cinema
Household, Maintenance Products
and Pet Products
p.178/179

De Franse keuken voor katten.

Van Gogh

Advertising Agency
Ogilvy & Mather, Paris
Client
Avi
Creative Director
Bernard Bureau
Copywriter
Franck Rey
Art Director
Stéphanie Surer
Agency Producer
Nicole Bacquer
Production Company
Telema, Levallois-Perret
Producer
Corinne Lizarraga
Director
Etienne Chatiliez

We see a beautiful, almost dreamy decor, recently repainted a brilliant colour.
>In the room, two masterpieces are hanging on the wall. Suddenly, they start to move and to speak as experts about the quality of the paint that was used to redo the wall where they had once hung.
>One of the works symbolizes the cubist's movement. The other is a self-portrait of Vincent Van Gogh, one ear cut off. This handicap illustrates that he does not hear very well.
"What do you think of the new paint job?"
"What?"
"They repainted with Avi paint."
"Yellow does show the dirt."
"True, but it's washable."
"What?"
"Nothing."
"I did hear that with Avi it takes just one coat, dries in thirty minutes, and there's no smell."
"And you can clean your brushes with water."
"What?"
"You really should get your ears tested."

Open on shot of stormy Paris.
>Thunder crashing in background.
>A wall featuring Eric Cantona
is seen.
>We see a´ ball flying past the
Eiffel tower.
>Noise of ball flying with rocket
like speed.
>Close up of the Cantona Wall.
The ball flies into the picture.
He beats an opponent and kicks
the ball, destroying a part of
the wall with his shot.
>Crowd cheering. Noise of power
kick. Brick smashing.
>The ball flies past the
Brandenberg gate to a wall in
Berlin featuring Michael Schulz.
>Noise of fast moving ball.
Crowd cheering.
>Schulz takes the ball on his
chest, dribbles for a couple of
steps and passes the ball,
destroying part of the wall.
>Noise of ball being kicked.
Noise of bricks smashing.
>The ball flies to a city in
Italy, upsetting some pigeons,
where Maldini comes to life on
his wall and heads the ball
back to London. Bricks fly from
the wall.
>Fast moving ball noise. Pigeon
wings flapping. Noise of header.
Bricks smashing.
>Shot of London.
>Fast moving ball noise.
>Ian Wright kicks the ball from
his wall, past the Tower Bridge,
removing some bricks with his
kick.
>Bricks smashing.
>The ball flies across the ocean
to Brazil and into Rio de Janiero
where Romario and Bebeto are seen
on two side by side walls.
>Romario heads the ball to Bebeto
who kicks it to Mexico where
Campos dives across
three buildings to catch it.
>Smashing bricks. Moving ball.
Kicking sound and more smashing
bricks.
>Campos dislodges a Nike logo
with his arms on the third
building. The sign swings loose
from one corner.
>Moving ball. Crash of broken
glass as he hits logo. Sound of
swinging.
Nike

Eurobest Award Winner
The Wall
Advertising Agency
Wieden & Kennedy, Amsterdam
Client
Nike Europe
Creative Director
Dan Wieden/Susan Hoffman
Copywriter
Bob Moore
Art Director
Warren Eakins
Agency Producer
Jane Brimblecombe
Production Company
Pytka Productions, Venice, Cal.
Director
Joe Pytka
Sound
Sony Pictures: Albert Ibbotson

Television and Cinema
Clothing, Footwear and
Accessories
p.180/181

Open on storeman reading
newspaper in a quiet magazine
store.
>We hear sound of newspaper
pages rustling.
>Jim Courier comes to life on
the cover of a tennis magazine
and smashes a backhand.
>Noise of racquet hitting ball
and Courier exhaling as he hits
ball. Sound of ball zooming
through air.
>Agassi stretches for a forehand
from the cover of Tennis Match
magazine.
>Agassi's racquet hitting ball.
>John McEnroe ducks as the ball
clips the magazine where he is
featured on the cover.
A card falls out of the magazine.
>Ball clipping magazine and card
dropping onto the shelf.
>The storeman looks up from his
newspaper.
>Rustle of newspaper pages.
>McEnroe climbs up his magazine
cover trying to get a better
view.
"What the..."
Pioline returns the ball with a
backhand.
>Grunt as Pioline hits the ball
and the noise of the racquet
hitting the ball.
>Krajicek smashes ball.
>Noise of a fast moving ball.
Noise of Krajicek hitting ball.
>Ball flies past Bride magazine
and surprises bride on cover.
>Pioline turns to follow the
path of the ball.
>Glass breaking.
>Gabby catches ball with one
hand.
>Ball being caught. Audience
applauding.
>The store owner begins to get
out of his chair.
>Gabby throws ball out of
magazine. A ball boy appears
from behind a stand and
retrieves the ball.
>Linesman calling "Fault".
Running footsteps.
>Storeman enters room with a
dustpan and broom.
>The pages of a tennis magazine
flick over as the players in the
photographs play out a point.
>Players grunting as they hit
the ball and the sound of
racquets hitting ball. Pages of
a magazine flicking over.
>The ball flies to an art
magazine and smashes the plate
on the cover.
>Loud grunt, ball flying through
air and glass smashing.
>Courier/Krajicek face camera.
"Shhhh."
Storeman cleans up the broken
glass.
Nike

Eurobest Award Winner
Magazine Wars
Advertising Agency
Wieden & Kenndey, Amsterdam
Client
Nike Europe
Creative Director
Dan Wieden/Bob Moore
Copywriter
Evelyn Monroe
Art Director
Susan Hoffman
Agency Producer
Jane Brimblecombe
Production Company
Propaganda, Los Angeles
Director
David Fincher
Sound Design
Ren Klyce

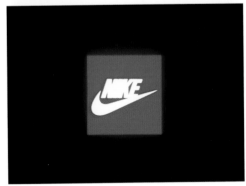

Television and Cinema
Clothing, Footwear and
Accessories
p.182/183

Alpvillage
Advertising Agency
**Paradiset DDB Needham,
Stockholm**
Client
Diesel
Creative Director
Joakim Jonason
Copywriter
Linus Karlsson
Art Director
Joakim Jonason
Production Company
Mod:Film, Stockholm
Director
Terence O'Connor/Marek Losey
Music
Miller Williams/Yount Harris

A man walks through an alpine
village with his cow. During his
walk he meets a variety of
people. A thirteen year old
devil drinking beer, a bunny
girl, Santa Claus, an Engelbert
Humperdink look-alike, a sado-
masochistic work-out group. The
young devil finally gets crushed
by a phoney ten thousand ton
weight which falls on him. The
man with the cow leaves the
village.
**For successful living. Diesel
Jeans & Workwear**

Magic 55
Advertising Agency
Paradiset DDB Needham,
Stockholm
Client
Diesel
Creative Director
Joakim Jonason
Copywriter
Linus Karlsson
Art Director
Joakim Jonason
Production Company
Mod:Film, Stockholm
Director
Jhoan Camitz
Music
Tom Wolgers

A washing detergent commercial which looks like any other washing detergent commercial on T.V. It differs from other commercials in that the results achieved from using Magic 55 are greatly exaggerated. The commercial takes place in Tokyo and Japanese is spoken throughout. We discover at the end that it is in fact a commercial for jeans. **For successful living. Diesel Jeans & Workwear**

Bald Man
Advertising Agency
Young & Rubicam Portugal, Lisbon
Client
MBB Teixeira
Creative Director
Edson Athayde
Copywriter
Edson Athayde/Leandro Alvarez
Art Director
Cássio Moron
Agency Producer
Sandra Ribeiro
Production Company
Metrópole Filmes
Director
Sérgio Henriques

Television and Cinema
Clothing, Footwear and
Accessories/
Cosmetic, Beauty Products and
Perfume
p.184/185

A bald man who has only a little
tuft of hair talks to the camera
with the Bel Hair products in front
of him.
"This is the new Bel Hair line
for those who love to change their
hair-do."
>The bald man starts to change
his hair according to the voice.
"Increase the body, stick it up,
stress the curls or, if you wish,
change it from one
side...to the other."
>Cut to pack-shot of all the Bel
Hair line.
"Bel Hair. Different hair every
day."
Cut to bald man just as he started
the film, flirting with the camera.
"Today I've put it all backwards,
à la Clark Gable."
Bel Hair

Legman

Advertising Agency
Bartle Bogle Hegarty, London
Client
Levi Strauss & Co. Europe
Creative Director
John Hegarty
Copywriter
John O'Keefe
Art Director
Russell Ramsay
Agency Producer
Philippa Crane
Production Company
Arden Sutherland-Dodd, London
Producer
Nancy Amster-Coull
Director
Paul Arden
Lighting Cameraman
Stephen Goldblatt
Music
Fall

It's the 1940's.
>A young oil worker falls from a
rig and is taken to hospital.
>A young nurse looks on as an
older nurse goes to his aid.
>In the treatment room, she can
tell he's badly injured, so
takes out her scissors to cut
his jeans off. He refuses to let
her cut his 501s so, very
gently, she undoes his buttons.
>All this is witnessed through
the door by the younger nurse.
The tension between the trio as
the older nurse pulls off his
jeans is broken by the entrance
of an old, officious looking
doctor. He flicks disapproving
looks at the patient and nurse.
**1944 Wartime. Levi's 501 jeans
in short supply.**

Kookaï Perfum IV
Advertising Agency
CLM/BBDO, Issy les Moulineaux
Client
Gemey Paris
Creative Director
Benoit Devarrieux
Copywriter
Dominique Quessada
Art Director
Philippe Chanet
Agency Producer
Virginie Meldener
Production Company
PAC, Neuilly sur Seine
Producer
Thierry de Ganay
Director
Patrick Bouchitey

A pretty young girl whom we see only from the waist up, has her back to the camera.
She is wearing a fairly see-through, black, low-cut bustier which is exposing one shoulder. She turns round to face the camera and, spraying perfume onto herself, she says:
"I'm sure I am contributing to the rise in the planet's temperature."
She seems sure of herself, cheeky, sensual. Then, turning back round, she removes her bustier uncovering her breasts, of which we catch a glimpse.
Kookaï Parfums — Paris.

Television and Cinema
Cosmetic, Beauty Products and Perfume
p.186/187

Kookaï Perfum V
Advertising Agency
CLM/BBDO, Issy les Moulineaux
Client
Gemey Paris
Creative Director
Benoit Devarrieux
Copywriter
Dominique Quessada
Art Director
Philippe Chanet
Agency Producer
Virginie Meldener
Production Company
PAC, Neuilly sur Seine
Producer
Thierry de Ganay
Director
Patrick Bouchitey

A pretty young girl, whom we
see only from the waist up, is
swinging her hips in a sensual
manner. She is dressed only in
a bra and says:
"Boys fitted with heart
pacemakers are advised to avoid
watching this film."
Then she dances confidently,
cheekily, pouting and spraying
perfume on herself several
times.
Kookaï Parfums — Paris.

Eurobest Award Winner
Packet
Client
Johnson & Johnson
Creative Director
Paul Arden
Copywriter
Paul Arden
Art Director
Paul Arden
Production Company
Arden Sutherland-Dodd, London
Producer
Nick Sutherland-Dodd
Director
Paul Arden
Lighting Cameraman
Jan Richter-Friis
Music
Jenkins Ratledge

The film opens on a Mates condom
packet resting on a sheet.
>The camera begins to move in
and out on the motionless pack,
accompanied by music which
slowly rises to a crescendo.
>The film ends with a long zoom
in to a close-up of the pack.
Mates Ultra Safe.

Hippie
Advertising Agency
New Deal DDB Needham, Oslo
Client
Nycomed Pharma
Copywriter
Erik Hersoug
Art Director
Morten Kristiansen
Production Company
Big Deal, Oslo
Producer
Turid Øversveen
Director
Pål Sletaune

A 'survivor' from the hippie era
is asleep in bed. Due to the
light outside and the church
bells we understand that it is
mid-day. The hippie awakes,
grabs his guitar by the bed and
starts singing:
"When I woke up this morning..."
He collapses, puts the guitar
away and falls back in the bed.
He falls asleep immediately.

"Today we draw the teacher"

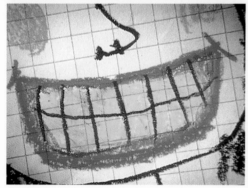

Don't be the last one to realize that you need it.

Teacher
Advertising Agency
Contrapunto, Madrid
Client
Cederroth
Creative Director
Juan Mariano Mancebo/
Ana Hidalgo
Copywriter
Julio Wallovits
Art Director
Jorge Lopez
Agency Producer
Luis Felipe Moreno
Production Company
Nucleo, Madrid
Producer
Luis Felipe Moreno
Director
Francisco Acuses
Lighting Cameraman
Fernando Rodriguez

During the break a teacher is
studying the pictures that her
pupils have drawn.
>The exercise of the day was to
draw the teacher.
>The teacher is looking amused,
but suddenly she realizes that
all the kids have drawn her with
a yellow toothed smile.
Whitening Dentabrit. Don't be
the last one to realize that you
need it.

Pill
Advertising Agency
Delvico Bates Barcelona
Client
Herbora
Creative Director
Toni Segarra/
Félix Fernandez de Castro
Copywriter
Javier Carro
Art Director
David Caballero
Agency Producer
Javier Carro
Production Company
Ovideo TV, Barcelona
Producer
Pepo Sol
Director
Sergi Piera

A couple in the park. Suddenly
the woman exclaims:
"I've forgotten to take the pill
again! Ohhh!"
"Children, we're going home!"
>A lot of children appear from
everywhere in the park.
Fosfomen. A nutritional
supplement for memory problems.

GUHL, JE TWEEDE NATUUR.

Second Nature
Advertising Agency
Campaign Company, Amsterdam
Client
Guhl Ikebana
Copywriter
Lysbeth Bijlstra
Art Director
Béla Stamenkovits
Production Company
**Directors Film Company,
New York**
Producer
Richard Coll
Director
Béla Stamenkovits
Music
Ramon Tiernagan

The film begins with a shot of a
girl in a landscape with a very
high hairdo.
>The camera moves to the side
and what one thought was her
hair, is in fact a cypress
tree.
>This scene is followed by
several others, including a palm
tree, a cloud and high grass.
>Packshot starts with one
bottle, camera moves to the
side, revealing different
bottles of Guhl haircare
products.
**Guhl haircare. Your second
nature.**

Television and Cinema
Toileries and Pharmaceuticals
p.192/193

AGAINST
THE
HORROR
OF
HAEMORRHOIDS
USE

Monsters

Advertising Agency
Young & Rubicam Portugal, Lisbon
Client
Whitehall
Creative Director
Edson Athayde
Copywriter
Edson Athayde/Jorge Teixeira
Art Director
Jorge Barrote
Agency Producer
Bruno Pinhal
Production Company
Lisboa Capital, Lisbon
Director
Diamantino Ferreira

Horror movie music.
>Several images of classic
monstrous characters are shown
accompanied by exclamations
of horror.
>The screams of horror increase at
the sight of a chair.
>Sounds of relief are heard when a
pack of Sperti Preparacao H is
shown.
"Against the horror of
haemorrhoids use Sperti-H pack."
"Or..."
A bicycle seat appears on the
screen and again we hear terrified
exclamations.

Slap
Advertising Agency
**GRAMM Advertising Agency,
Düsseldorf**
Client
Volvo Cars Europe Marketing
Creative Director
Dieter Grubitzsch
Copywriter
Frank Offermanns
Art Director
Oliver Popp
Production Company
Markenfilm & Co., Hamburg
Producer
Lutz Lobmaier
Director
Patrick Morgan
Lighting Cameraman
David Norton
Music
David Dundas

A presenter faces the camera and
slaps himself hard on the left
cheek.
"Every fourth car accident
happens from the left..."
He slaps himself on the right.
"...or the right."
Slow motion replay in a close-
up. He looks ruffled for a
moment and straightens up again.
"That's why Volvo has improved
its Protection-System SIPS..."
He fills up his left cheek with
air and hits himself again. The
blown up cheek softens the
impact of his hand
significantly.
"...with the SIPS-BAG."
He does the same trick with his
right cheek.
"The airbag on your side."
The presenter is now sitting in
a Volvo seat. A demo explosion
triggers the SIPS-BAG on his
side.
"In your seat."
The camera pulls back. The
presenter has doubled and is now
also sitting on the passengers
side. A SIPS-BAG explodes.
"On both sides."
"SIPS-BAG. The first on your
side."
"By Volvo."
Volvo.

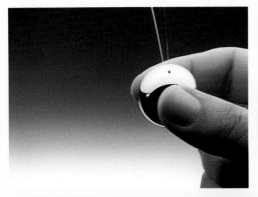
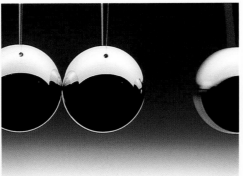
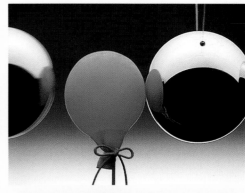

VOLVO

Eurobest Award Winner
Pendulum
Advertising Agency
**GRAMM Advertising Agency,
Düsseldorf**
Client
Volvo Cars Europe Marketing
Creative Director
Dieter Grubitzsch
Copywriter
Bernd Grellmann
Art Director
Ingo Waclawczyk
Production Company
Markenfilm & Co., Hamburg
Producer
Lutz Lobmaier
Director
Patrick Morgan
Lighting Cameraman
David Norton
Music
David Dundas

Five balls hanging on threads.
>The ball on the far right is
pulled to the right and released
onto the others.
"Every fourth car accident
happens from the side."
The ball on the right bangs
against the next closest one,
sending the ball on the far left
in motion.
"That's why Volvo has SIPS — a
system that transfers the
energy..."
Slow motion replay.
"...away from the impact."
Back to the first situation
where the balls are hanging
freely.
"Now Volvo has added a new
dimension."
Now the two balls on the right
are released onto the others.
"The SIPS-BAG!"
In slow motion a close up shows
a party balloon coming up next
to the middle ball to protect it
from the impact.
"The first airbag that protects
your weakest side."
Now the balls on the left come
towards the ball in the centre,
where a second party balloon
comes up.
"Or that of your passenger."
The SIPS-BAG logo explodes.
"SIPS-BAG, the first on your
side."
A SIPS-BAG explodes on the
driver's seat.
"In your seat."
A SIPS-BAG explodes on the
passenger's seat.
"By Volvo."
Volvo.

SEE A DIFFERENT WORLD.

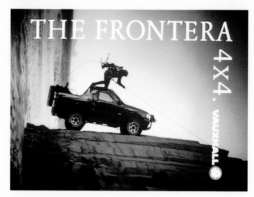

THE FRONTERA 4X4. VAUXHALL

The World According To Frontera
Advertising Agency
Lowe Howard-Spink, London
Client
Vauxhall Motor Company
Creative Director
Paul Weinberger
Copywriter
Phil Dearman
Art Director
Charles Inge
Agency Producer
Charles Crisp
Production Company
Paul Weiland Film Company, London
Producer
Paul Rothwell
Director
Frank Budgen
Lighting Cameraman
Henry Braham
Music
David Motion

Languid, mysterious and beautiful music is playing.
>We open on a close-up of two African women with water jugs apparently standing at an impossible 45 degree angle — on the horizon a Frontera is driving past them, apparently straight ahead.
>We dissolve to a close-up of the Frontera travelling through water which is at an odd 45 degree angle. We pull out to reveal Philippino fishermen on poles in the water. They are apparently at an impossible 45 degree angle as the Frontera drives past them through the water.
>We cut to the car driving in front of a waterfall with the water running at a 45 degree angle behind it.
>We see a close-up of Mongolian horsemen leading their horses down a slope. We see horsemen and horses oddly angled to the horizon. The Frontera passes them apparently on the level. However, pulling back reveals that the horizon they are on is not level at all but in reality a steep slope.
>We cut to a Frontera parked facing downhill on a 45 degree ice-covered slope.
>We cut to a sleigh with Eskimo children sliding past the Frontera, apparently going up hill.
"See a different world."
We cut to a winch mechanism winching itself up. Cut to reveal the Frontera being winched up, suspended in mid-air.
>We cut to a climber abseiling down the rock face which is angled horizontally. A Frontera, which is hanging from a winch rope, sits horizontally as if on a real horizon.
Frontera 4 x 4.

Roads
Advertising Agency
Contrapunto, Madrid
Client
Rover Spain
Creative Director
Juan Mariano Mancebo/
Ana Hidalgo
Copywriter
Julio Wallovits
Art Director
Jorge Lopez
Agency Producer
Luis Felipe Moreno
Production Company
Nucleo, Madrid
Producer
Luis Felipe Moreno
Director
Ramon Corominas

A view of a desert.
"Wouldn't it be great if the
Government built all of the
highways that they promised to?"
Another image of the same desert.
"No."
Land Rover.

Swedish Cartest I

Advertising Agency
Wibroe Duckert & Partners, Copenhagen

Client
Mazda Denmark

Copywriter
Stein Leikanger

Art Director
Bent Baerentzen

Agency Producer
Gitte Soerensen

Production Company
Easy Film, Copenhagen

Producer
Martin Elley

Director
Stein Leikanger

Lighting Cameraman
Tomas Boman

Music
Nicolai Egelund

At the Swedish Cartest Institute, Lennart and his test crew are having a hard time finding errors on the Mazda 626. "Have you found something?" "No, we have found nothing." "But you must find something..." "I haven't found anything, either..." "The shock absorbers?" "I've checked every damn part!" "Oh no — there must be something to find..." "Uhhh, find something!" The phone suddenly rings. It's Lennart's wife: "Hello — no sweetie, I won't be coming home tonight — I must find something." **Mazda 626. The car with the fewest errors. Swedish Cartest Institute.**

Volkswagen. Who else?

The Golf Variant from Volkswagen.

What Would You Like?
Advertising Agency
DDB Needham Worldwide, Amsterdam
Client
Pon's Automobielhandel
Creative Director
Lode Schaeffer/Erik Wünsch
Copywriter
Erik Wünsch
Art Director
Lode Schaeffer

The new Volkswagen Golf Variant

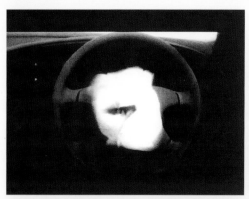
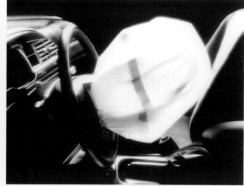

Standaard airbag op elke Ford.

Uitgezonderd Maverick.

Airbag
Advertising Agency
Ogilvy & Mather Amsterdam
Client
Ford Nederland
Creative Director
Krijn van Noordwijk
Copywriter
Krijn van Noordwijk
Art Director
Krijn van Noordwijk
Agency Producer
Rosemarie Praaning
Producer
Rosemarie Praaning
Director
Krijn van Noordwijk
Music
Reinder van Zalk

With the sound of a crash, an
airbag bursts out of a Ford
steering-wheel.
>We see the airbag make the
throbbing movements of a human
heart.
>We also hear the sound of a
heart beating.
Standard Airbag on every Ford.

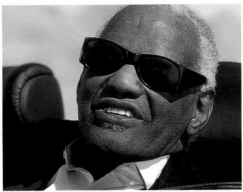

Quand on la voit on la veut.

PEUGEOT

LAC SALÉ - USA

Eurobest Award Winner
Ray Charles
Advertising Agency
Euro RSCG Babinet Tong Cuong &
Associés, Levallois-Perret
Client
Automobiles Peugeot
Copywriter
Bertrand Delaire
Art Director
François Serres
Agency Producer
Arnaud Granier-Deferre
Production Company
Hamster Publicité, Suresnes
Producer
Jean-Jacques Grimblat
Director
Gerard Pires
Lighting Cameraman
Alex Thomson
Music
'Georgia': Ray Charles

Music — 'Georgia' sung by Ray
Charles.
>We see Ray Charles driving a
Peugeot 306 Convertible in Salt
Lake, USA.
To see it is to want it.
Peugeot.

Rover 600.
The Gentleman's
Automobile.

De Rover 600 vanaf 42.900,-

We see a distinguished, middle-aged gentleman close up.
"You just don't lend your Rover 600 to your son..."
We see the man nodding, apparently in agreement. The camera zooms out slowly and we see a Rover 600 to the right of him.
"...unless..."
We hear keys clinking.
>As the camera zooms out further, it reveals that on the left of the man there is another gentleman of slighter build, and with thinning, grey hair, but otherwise quite similar. This man is making threatening gestures with the keys that he is holding (just out of reach of the first man)...
"...unless he's CEO of a big company!"
The son tries to grab the keys.
>Rover 600 from f42.900,-
We hear muffled banging, followed by moaning, a car door slamming and the start of a Rover 600 engine.
>The son drives off, grinning (but with a black eye).
Rover 600
The Gentleman's Automobile.

Father & Son
Advertising Agency
KMM Amsterdam
Client
Rover
Copywriter
Marien Faber
Art Director
Erik Vos
Agency Producer
Esther Verksaik
Production Company
Not Just Film, Amsterdam
Producer
Aart Villerius
Director
Paolo Pistolesi
Lighting Cameraman
Joost von Storrenburg

Golf. Ⓥ

C'est pourtant facile de ne pas se tromper.

Birthday
Advertising Agency
DDB Needham France, Paris
Client
VAG France
Creative Director
Christian Vince
Copywriter
Gabriel Gauthier
Art Director
Hervé Riffault
Agency Producer
Philippe Garnier
Production Company
Summertime, Paris
Producer
Jean Marie Benard
Director
Hervé Hiole
Lighting Cameraman
Bernard Lutic
Music
Patty Mildred Hill

A voice-over announces:
"The Golf is twenty years old
this week ."
We see various mechanics who
reluctantly sing 'Happy
Birthday.'
"Twenty years without any
problems is a long time."
Golf. VW.

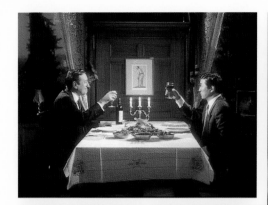

Nya Toyota Carina E.
Precisionsbyggd
i England.

TOYOTA

A British Toyota manager has
invited a Japanese Toyota
business friend to dinner. He
toasts his friend's arrival:
"Welcome to Bolton."
He then hands him some
chopsticks:
"I think you'll recognise these.
From Tokyo."
The Japanese man recognises them
as a gift which he had given the
Englishman on a previous
occasion.
>The Englishman goes on to
relate an earlier discussion he
has had with his wife concern-
ing what type of food to serve
at dinner.
"I said, Pauline, there is no
way I'm inviting a Japanese
friend of mine over here, and
giving him sushi. That would be
like taking coals to Newcastle."
A fly is heard buzzing in the
background. The Englishman
continues the conversation with
the next problem to be solved;
knives and forks or chopsticks?
"I said, Pauline, there is
absolutely no way I'm inviting a
Japanese friend of mine over
here and expecting him to eat
with a knife and fork."
At this point, the Englishman
catches the fly with his
chopsticks demonstrating that he
has learnt the Japanese
technique perfectly.
"Because I know you would find
it very difficult to eat with a
knife and fork."
**All new Toyota Carina E.
Precision Built in England.**

Chopsticks
Advertising Agency
Alinder & Co., Stockholm
Client
Toyota Autoimport
Creative Director
Mats Alinder
Copywriter
Stefan Rönnquist
Art Director
Mats Alinder
Production Company
Thorne Film, Stockholm
Producer
Josh Thorne
Director
Colin Nutley
Lighting Cameraman
Jörgen Persson

We open on a stunt man running
towards the camera.
"I used to be a stunt kid before
I was a stunt man."
We cut to the stunt man standing
on scaffolding.
"I learned one thing early on —
belief is everything."
We cut to footage of the stunt
man as a child.
"My interest in cars started on
my fourth birthday...I've loved
driving cars ever since."
We cut to the stunt man driving
a Volvo.
"That's why I like this car —
it's great to drive."
We cut to a close-up of the
stunt man on the bridge.
"I've never been afraid of
heights. I guess I have a pretty
healthy fear of death."
He calculates the risks of the
dangerous stunt he is about to
perform.
"One centimetre this way or that
and it's four hundred miles
down."
He describes the beauty of
driving the Volvo.
"When I ask it to do something
it responds. Control, I'm a
control freak."
We see him perform the stunt
successfully.
"You know, some people say I'll
believe it when I see it. I
prefer to say you'll see it
when you believe it."
We cut to a close-up of the
stunt man standing up in a
shopping trolley.
"They think my stunts are
crazy."
Volvo

The Stuntman
Advertising Agency
Abbott-Mead Vickers.BBDO, London
Client
Volvo
Copywriter
Tom Carty
Art Director
Walter Campbell
Agency Producer
Lindsay Hughes
Production Company
Tony Kaye Films, London
Producer
Yvonne Chalk/Miranda Davis
Director
Tony Kaye
Lighting Cameraman
Tony Kaye
Music
Tony Kaye

amazing

maZDa

Tornado
Advertising Agency
PMSvW/Y&R, Amsterdam
Client
Autopalace de Binckhorst
Creative Director
Karel Beyen
Copywriter
Karel Beyen
Art Director
Martin Cornelissen
Agency Producer
Marijke Kolsteeg
Production Company
Thed Lenssen Film, Amsterdam
Producer
Ronald Hietbrink
Director
Benjamin Landshoff
Lighting Cameraman
Benjamin Landshoff
Music
Wim Vonk Sound Productions

Television and Cinema
Automotive/
Automotive Accessories
p.208/209

When a tornado hits a parking
lot, all the cars are blown away
except one: the Mazda with
amazing roadholding.
Mazda.

Open on a black Toyota Supra, beautifully lit in a studio. The camera slowly explores its curvy lines: we see the headlights, the wheel arches, the rake of the bonnet.

>From above in slow motion, several hundred gallons of green paint pour down covering the car.

"From now on all performance cars are green."

A series of close ups show the paint dripping down the windows, over the headlights and over the car badge.

>Cut to a black Rover 600. Several hundred gallons of silver paint splash down covering the car.

"Modern cars, silver."

Cut to a black Peugeot Estate. Suddenly, gallons of dark blue paint pour down.

"Family cars, dark blue."

Cut to a black Peugeot 306 diesel again beautifully lit. This time, gallons of red paint pour down.

"Diesels are red..."

Cut to a black VW Beetle.

As the camera moves around, several hundred gallons of light blue paint pours down.

"...and older cars are light blue."

Cut to a close-up on a black pack-shot large in frame. Green paint pours down to create the Ultron pack.

"Esso quality oils are colour coded."

Camera pulls wider to include four other black packs. In quick succession paint pours down over them creating the rest of the Esso range.

"So choosing the right oil has never been so simple."

Esso Simple.

Paint

Advertising Agency
J Walter Thompson, London
Client
Esso
Creative Director
Jaspar Shelbourne
Copywriter
Andrew Singleton
Art Director
Jono Wardle
Agency Producer
Paul Fenton
Production Company
Produktion, London
Producer
Bruce Williamson
Director
Martin Brierley
Lighting Cameraman
Keith Goddard

The Fork Lift
Advertising Agency
McCann-Erickson, Oslo
Client
Glassbransjeforbundet
Art Director
Jan Erik Rönning
Production Company
Dynamit Film, Bromma
Producer
Bamse Ulfung
Director
Rickard Petrelius
Lighting Cameraman
Stefan Kullänger
Music
Gunnar Wennborg

A beautiful secretary leaves the office of a warehouse. Workers are installing a new window.
>The secretary goes out to the warehouse and passes a man driving a fork-lift truck. He whistles and gives her yearning looks.
>He loses his concentration while driving. Travelling full speed, he slams into the new window.
>The glass doesn't break, but the fork-lift truck bends with the impact.
Safety Glass. Can Stand a Fork-Lift. Federation of Glass Trade.

Trafikk ute - musikk inne
STØYDEMPENDE GLASS

Trafikk ute - musikk inne
STØYDEMPENDE GLASS
GLASSBRANSJEFORBUNDET

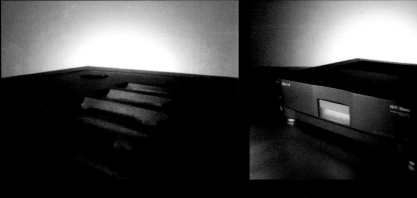

BESTE KOOP IN DE CONSUMENTENGIDS

Four Smartheads
Advertising Agency
PMSvW/Y&R, Amsterdam

We see the camera panning over
the top of a Sony video
recorder.

No Smoking
Advertising Agency
Sek & Grey, Helsinki
Client
Canon
Copywriter
Pekka Laurikainen
Art Director
Esko Moilanen
Production Company
Oh-la-la Filmproduction, Stockholm
Director
Olavi Häkkinen
Lighting Cameraman
Jörgen Persson/Danne Myhrman

Television and Cinema
Business Equipment and Services/
Gift, Luxury and Tobacco Items
p.216/217

Two strangers share a table in an airport lounge. One is about to smoke a cigarette but notices there is no ashtray, so he goes away to get one. The second man sees this from behind his newspaper and quickly opens his Canon Notebook PC on the table. He strikes a few keys, and a sheet of paper rolls out of the computer. He takes the sheet, folds it and places it standing up on the table. Displaying a No Smoking text and symbol, the sheet now looks like a genuine warning sign. The first man now returns with an ashtray, sits down, puts a cigarette in his mouth — and freezes as he sees the sign. He looks puzzled. The non-smoker hides behind his newspaper as if nothing has happened.
Canon.

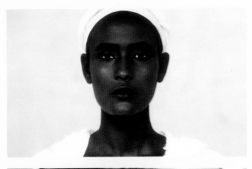

Pomellato
Advertising Agency
McCann-Erickson, Milan
Client
Pomellato
Creative Director
Milka Pogliani
Agency Producer
Lorella Stortini
Production Company
BRW & Partners, Milan
Producer
Daniela Cattaneo
Director
Fatima Andrade
Lighting Cameraman
Larry Fong
Music
'Yulunga': Dad Can Dance

The story takes place on the island of Male, an extraordinary setting amidst the waters and mud banks near Timbucktu. Only a very young prince can manage to bring back a smile to a beautiful, but very sad-looking young girl who refuses the precious gifts offered to her by wealthy admirers, seeing ahead of her a future of solitude and desolation. His gift is a Pomellato ring.

Sledge
Advertising Agency
New Deal DDB Needham, Oslo
Client
Norsk Tipping
Copywriter
Ivar Vereide
Art Director
Ingvar Moi
Production Company
Big Deal, Oslo
Producer
Turid Øversveen
Director
Marius Holst
Lighting Cameraman
Philip Øgaard

It's a beautiful winter morning
in the woods. A horse and sledge
are approaching on a snow-
covered road. It stops at a red
light.
>In the sledge we see an elderly
rich millionaire covered with
furs. Facing him are his twin
grandsons who are obviously not
enjoying themselves.
>Suddenly one of the grandsons
is hit by a snowball. At the
same time another sledge pulls
up beside them.
>A huge man, dressed like Davy
Crockett, is bending forward.
Facing him are triplets dressed
in identical outfits who are
obviously enjoying themselves.
>As they pull away we see that
their sledge is an old Ford
Anglia converted to a stretch
limo on skis, drawn by four
horses.
>There are millionaires — and
then there are Lotto-
millionaires!

Sheep
Advertising Agency
New Deal DDB Needham, Oslo
Client
Norsk Tipping
Copywriter
Ivar Vereide
Art Director
Ingvar Moi
Production Company
Moland Film, Oslo
Producer
Irene Sødal Dietrichson
Director
Marius Holst
Lighting Cameraman
John Christian Rosenlund

We are at an exclusive hairdresser — for dogs. Preferably
poodles with a 'lion-style'
haircut.
>A bunch of snobbish, healthy
looking customers are fondling
their dogs and drinking tea,
waiting for 'Fido' to be served.
>Suddenly a pair of muddy boots
appear on the clean carpet. All
the affluent people stop
whatever they're doing and look
at the person in horror and
disbelief. All the dogs start
panicking.
>We cut to a sweet old lady, a
typical farmers wife, smiling
happily to everyone around
her. Beside her is her favourite
sheep — with a 'lion-style'
haircut, exactly like the
poodles. Proudly she walks out
of the room.

Eurobest Award Winner
Europe's Theatre
Advertising Agency
Opera-RLC, Paris
Client
Théâtre de L'Odéon
Creative Director
Anne de Maupeou
Copywriter
Jocelyn Devaux
Art Director
Anne Zaslavsky
Agency Producer
Frédéric Rippert
Production Company
Summertime, Paris
Producer
Jean-Marie Benard
Director
Hervé Hiolle
Lighting Cameraman
Sabine Lancelin
Music
Hugues le Bars

"The Italians have very decided
views about the Germans."
"As the English have about the
Italians."
"Or the Spaniards about the
English."
"Or even the French about the
Spaniards."
"It's high time that Europeans
got to know other Europeans
better."
Odéon — Théâtre de l'Europe.

Television and Cinema
Leisure and Entertainment
p.220/221

Les Mamies
Advertising Agency
BDDP, Boulogne
Client
La Francaise des Jeux
Creative Director
Marie-Catherine Dupuy/
Jean-Pierre Barbou
Copywriter
Bruno Lacoste
Art Director
Antoine Barthuel
Agency Producer
Evelyne Luverdis
Production Company
Premiere Heure, Paris
Producer
Richard Jacobs
Director
Valérie Lemercier

Two ladies enter a shop intent
on buying a lottery ticket.
They speak at once.
"I'd like a Tacotac please."
There is confusion as to who
asked first.
"Go ahead."
"No, please you were before me."
"Are you sure."
"Yes, I insist."
One of them scratches the ticket
and is unsuccessful but the
second time she proves to be
much more successful:
"Two million, thank you."
The lady leaves the shop elated,
leaving the other lady looking
suitably disappointed:
"Don't mention it."
Tacotac.

Collegues De Bureau
Advertising Agency
BDDP, Boulogne
Client
La Francaise des Jeux
Creative Director
**Marie-Catherine Dupuy/
Jean-Pierre Barbou**
Copywriter
Bruno Lacoste
Art Director
Antoine Barthuel
Agency Producer
Evelyne Luverdis
Production Company
Premiere Heure, Paris
Producer
Richard Jacobs
Director
Valérie Lemercier

Two colleagues are having a
coffee together.
"Can you keep your eye on my
Tacotac. I'm just going to the
toilet."
In his absence, his colleague
scratches the lottery ticket.
"Two hundred thousand francs."
He rushes to the bar and buys
another lottery ticket before
his colleague's return.
>Unaware of what has happened,
his colleague returns and
scratches his ticket to discover
he's won.
"Hey, twenty francs. The drinks
are on me."
Tacotac.

Mask

Advertising Agency	A woman is wearing a black
FCB Hamburg	leather corset and is sitting in
Client	front of a plate of food. We
Erotic Art Museum	hear a darkly sensuous sound
Creative Director	collage by the German cult band
Hermann Vaske	'Einstürzende Neubauten'
Copywriter	throughout the entire spot.
Hermann Vaske	>We see that the woman is also
Art Director	wearing a leather mask. This
Stephan Pfeiffer/	seems to have slipped her mind.
Reinhold Rahm/Markus Lehmann	Only when she tries to put a
Agency Producer	forkful of food into her mouth
Charles V. Bender	does she remember. So she
Production Company	resolutely unzips the mouthpiece
Laszlo Kadar Films, Hamburg	of her mask and starts to eat.
Producer	"Satisfy your appetite...at the
Markus Janowski	Erotic Art Museum in Hamburg."
Director	In front of the woman we see an
Hermann Vaske	erotic oil painting.
Music	**Erotic Art Museum Hamburg**
Einstürzende Neubauten	"Now with restaurant."

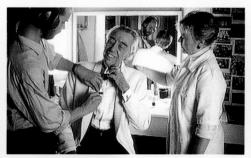

Leaving town
in a hurry?

We've got
lots of flights
going your way.

BRAATHENS S·A·F·E
- The Norwegian Airline.

The President and his men arrive
in the theatre.
>We cut to the dressing room
where the key speaker is
receiving a final touch-up of
make-up. A sound technician
enters and attaches a microphone
to the key speaker's collar,
then tests it for sound.
>The make-up artist asks the key
speaker:
"It must be a great honour for
you to welcome the President."
"Honour? Honour, my ass! He
looks and sounds just like Adolf
Hitler, ...but without the
charm."
We cut back to the theatre where
the key speaker's response is
broadcast and the President is
clearly angry. The audience
bursts out laughing.
>Next we see the key speaker on
board a plane. He squirms with
embarrassment.
>Background song lyrics: "Shame,
shame on you...shame, shame on
you"
"Leaving town in a hurry. We've
got lots of flights going your
way."
Braathens S.A.F.E.

The Dictator
Advertising Agency
Leo Burnett, Oslo
Client
Braathens SAFE Airline
Copywriter
Oistein Borge
Art Director
Johan Gulbranson
Production Company
Leo Film, Oslo
Producer
Knut E. Jensen/Anna Sohlman
Director
Johan Gulbranson
Lighting Cameraman
Thomas Boman
Music
Bohren & Aaserud

Rio
from
£299
return.

Where Is Everyone?
Advertising Agency
Saatchi & Saatchi, London
Client
British Airways
Creative Director
James Lowther/Simon Dicketts
Copywriter
Keith Bickel
Art Director
Carlos
Agency Producer
Tim Berriman
Production Company
Spots Films Services, London
Producer
Tim White
Director
Paul Meijer
Lighting Cameraman
Ivan Bird

This commercial is shot from camera point of view.
>Open on a man waking up in the morning.
>We hear the sound of a digital alarm clock.
>His hand reaches out and switches off the alarm. He throws an arm across the bed to reach for his wife. She's not there.
>He walks down the stairs and calls out.
"Carol!"
He looks in the kitchen but she's not there.
"Carol?"
He passes the goldfish tank and notices that the fish isn't there.
>The man leaves the house, climbs into his car and drives off.
>He drives through deserted streets, not a car or person in sight. He looks at his watch, it's 8.15 am, rush hour.
>He runs into a railway station. It's completely deserted.
>He looks in a cafe. There's no one there.
>He runs through more deserted streets desperately trying to find any sign of life.
>He runs up a flight of stairs and emerges into a large open-plan office. Again, there's nobody there at all, only his reflection in a mirror.
>In desperation he runs into the middle of a deserted street and screams.
"Where is everybody?!"
Rio from £299 return.
LA from £199 return.
Rome from £99 return.
Paris from £59 return.
New York from £168 return.
British Airways World Offers.

DAGEN ER
IKKE HELT DEN
SAMME
UTEN.

Toilet
Advertising Agency
New Deal DDB Needham, Oslo
Client
Verdens Gang
Copywriter
Ivar Vereide
Art Director
Morten Foss
Production Company
Big Deal, Oslo
Producer
Turid Øversveen
Director
Pål Sletaune
Lighting Cameraman
Kjell Vassdal

A man sits in a shabby old
bathroom looking bored and
despondent. He sits there trying
to find something to amuse
himself with. But there is
nothing to do except sit on the
toilet. Suddenly he looks at the
air-freshener. Very slowly he
bends over to check it out, then
realizes it's no fun at all and
falls back with resignation.
>Survival just ain't the same
without VG. Norway's favourite
daily.

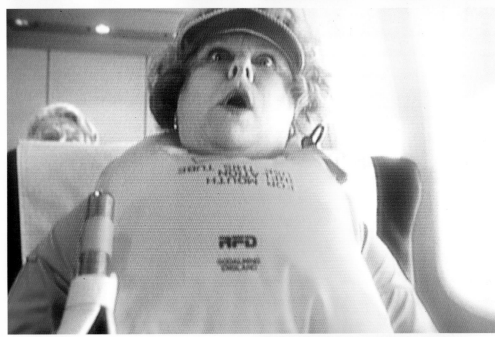

We are aboard a jet plane. The seat-belt sign has just been switched off signalling completion of take-off. Passengers release their belts and go about their business, while the stewardesses start their inflight catering routine.
>We hear the Captain over the PA system:
"Hello ladies and gentlemen. This is your Captain speaking. We have just reached our final cruising altitude of twenty thousand feet. Ahead of us is a cloudless sky and...know what? Today I'll do it — loop the loop!"
The aircraft goes into a dive and takes on speed. It banks a bit and begins to vibrate.
>The passengers panic and react in various comical ways.
"Yeah, I know — the engineers just don't believe this bird can hack it. But these ignoramuses have nothing but nuts and bolts in their heads. They have no idea what a man with a dream can do. Yes, a dream!"
"Okay, sure — anything can happen. But nothing beats that feeling of having given it a try at least once in your life. Right? Right!"
After a brief pause the Captain cracks up laughing.
"Just kidding, folks. 'Cause today we don't have Stern aboard, and I wanted to give you some thrilling entertainment nonetheless."
Back in the cockpit we see the co-pilot still looking flabbergasted at the Captain. The Captain pats his cheek reassuringly, as the steering column comes away in his hands.

Aircraft
Advertising Agency
Scholz & Friends, Hamburg
Client
Gruner & Jahr Verlag
Creative Director
Gerald Heinemann
Copywriter
Hans Albers
Art Director
Petra Mondwurf-Smid
Agency Producer
Sonja Dansmann
Production Company
Rose Hackney Productions, London
Producer
Bertie Miller
Director
Graham Rose
Lighting Cameraman
Jerry Dunkley

We open on typical black and white footage of Stalin's speech to the masses in the Red Square. The crowd are cheering. Behind him we see a bored club-circuit style drummer.
>In the style of a Northern stand-up comic Stalin says:
"...so the vicar says, No Mrs Pottersby, that's my chihuahua."
Cymbal crash.
>Silence.
>The crowd look solemn.
"Settle down, settle down... right, it's time I clamped down on things round 'ere. I'm scrappin' soccer for chess... that's good isn't it?"
Cymbal crash.
>Silence.
>We see a figure in the crowd wearing a football scarf. He looks disappointed.
>Stalin realises he's going down like a lead balloon and points to a man in the crowd wearing a silly Cossack hat.
"Hey you, are you wearing that hat for a bet?"
Cymbal crash.
>Even more silence.
>We see a row of women looking grim.
"Okay from now on there's only one type of knickers — itchy ones."
"And as for television, you'll all have to watch what I want to watch and only when I say so."
A man in the crowd heckles.
"Get off."
Silence.
"I'm only kiddin', show 'em Ivan."
We zoom-in close to an old-fashioned TV set and see a series of fast-paced Sky TV clips.
"With up to 20 channels of satellite television, you could watch more of what you want, Sky TV — there's no turning back. Freedom to choose."
>We zoom in even closer to see the Sky logo and No Turning Back end device.
>Crowd cheering.
"I've been Stalin, you've been wonderful. Thank you and good night."
Sky TV.

Stalin
Advertising Agency
Bartle Bogle Hegarty, London
Client
Sky
Creative Director
John Hegarty
Copywriter
Roger Beckett
Art Director
Andy Smart
Agency Producer
Rebecca Atkinson
Production Company
Limelight, London
Producer
David Botterill
Director
Daniel Kleinman
Lighting Cameraman
Ashley Rose

This is an ad for Z102

Z102 FM STOCKHOLM

Clapton
Advertising Agency
**Paradiset DDB Needham,
Stockholm**
Client
Z-Radio
Creative Director
Björn Rietz
Copywriter
Björn Rietz
Art Director
Paul Malmström
Production Company
Rally TV, Stockholm
Producer
Henrik Ihre
Director
Calle Åstrand

The commercial takes place in
complete silence. We see Eric
Clapton and band performing
live. Frequent close-ups on
Clapton's guitar as his fingers
rapidly move along the
fret-board.
"This is an ad for Z102 FM.
Right now we're playing one of
Clapton's hottest guitar solos.
If you want to listen to it,
turn your radio to 102 FM. NOW!"
Z102 FM Stockholm.

Dresden, Kansas

Amerika
Kreis Rochlitz
Freistaat Sachsen

Dresden/Amerika
Advertising Agency
Scholz & Friends, Berlin/ Dresden
Client
Dresdner Druck und Verlaghaus
Creative Director
Sebastian Turner
Copywriter
Joachim Schoepfer
Production Company
ZAK Film und Videoproduktion, Berlin
Producer
Martin Hagemann
Director
Ronald Eichhorn
Lighting Cameraman
Andreas Josimovic
Music
Arpad Bondy

Dresden is in America, Amerika is in East Germany. A paradox with which East German movie-goers and potential clients of the Dresdner newspaper Saechsishe Zeitung are confronted. The low budget commercial shows Americans, who live in small villages called Dresden in Ohio, Kansas, Tennessee and Ontario. The cast consists of inmates, a church choir, cowboys, policemen, firemen and many more. The text is partly improvised. (i.e: two old men in front of a gas station):
"This is my gas station."
"He's the mayor of Dresden."
"But who really gives a shit."
The final American scene shows a black 57 Chevy driving towards the camera. The screen turns black and we read: Nothing is more amazing than reality. Saechsische Zeitung. A black East German Trabant-vehicle passes the city limits of Amerika in Saxony. A little man standing next to the name sign of the town says in German:
"I am Hans and this is Saxony."

EAGLES

CATS

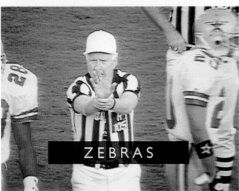

ZEBRAS

BUTTERFLIES

WASPS

HARES

Fauna
Advertising Agency
TBWA, Madrid
Client
Recoletos Compania Editorial
Creative Director
Alfonso Hernández/Andrés Alcalá
Copywriter
Alfonso Hernández
Art Director
Andrés Alcalá
Agency Producer
Pepe Carmona
Production Company
TBWA, Madrid
Director
Alfonso Hernández/Andrés Alcalá
Music
G. Donizetti

Eagles.
Cats.
Bantams.
Horses.
Grasshoppers.
Centipedes.
Zebras.
Butterflies.
Snakes.
Flamingos.
Wasps.
Hound Dogs.
Swans.
Hares.
Kangaroos.
Seals.
And of course
Athletes.
**In Marca, the Spanish Sports
Daily, Every Sport is Fair Game.**

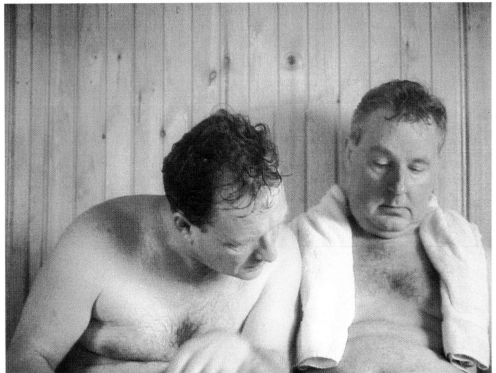

Sauna

Advertising Agency
Rönnberg McCann, Stockholm
Client
Expressen
Copywriter
Peter Kandimaa/Carl Lewenhaupt
Art Director
Mats Alinder
Production Company
**Oh-la-la Filmproduktion,
Stockholm**
Director
Olavi Häkkinen
Lighting Cameraman
Göran Nilsson

Two men sit in a sauna. One is
sleeping.
>The other guy is awake and
curiously glances into the lap
of the sleeping man.
>He giggles.
>Then he begins to study the lap
of the sleeping man.
>The sleeping man awakes and
stares at the curious man, then
invites him to take what he
wants from his lap. It out to
be Expressen newspaper.
**Sensations and Sensualism.
Expressen.**

TV Supplement
Advertising Agency
Rönnberg McCann, Stockholm
Client
Expressen
Copywriter
Peter Kandimaa
Art Director
Mats Alinder
Agency Producer
Mary Lee Copeland
Production Company
Lars Larsson Film, Stockholm
Producer
Lars Larsson
Director
Lars Larsson
Lighting Cameraman
Lars Larsson

A man adds the finishing touches
to his newly polished car.
>He stands back to admire it.
>A TV is thrown out of an
apartment window above.
>It crashes on top of his car.
>The man screams.
>He turns and kicks in the
apartment door.
Avoid painful programmes.
Read the new TV Expressen on
Thursdays.

Mr Bean, having just done his shopping, passes a Rema 1000 shop and sees the sign advertising lower prices.
>He goes in to check.
>Mr Bean is convinced that prices this low must mean that you get less than in other stores and starts checking against the goods he has bought in another shop.
>He checks to see if the loaves of bread are smaller...if the toothpaste tubes contain less toothpaste...and if there are less sweets in the bag sold at Rema 1000.
>After counting all the sweets he finds there is one more in his own bag.
>He rises triumphantly but then steps on the one sweet from the Rema 1000 bag that he has missed.
Same goods, same brands, lower prices. Rema 1000.

Just As Much
Advertising Agency
Markedskontakt, Trondheim
Client
Rema 1000
Copywriter
Alf Jentoft
Art Director
Finn S. Olderøyen
Production Company
The Film Factory, Oslo
Producer
Lasse Sæther/Roy Anderson
Director
Ingar Amundsen
Lighting Cameraman
Stein Holmberg
Music
**Jaques Offenbach/
Oistein Boassen**

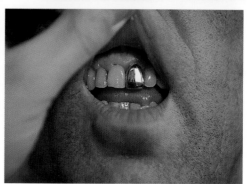

Radar
Advertising Agency
Markedskontakt, Trondheim
Client
Rema 1000
Copywriter
Alf Jentoft
Art Director
Finn S. Olderøyen
Production Company
The Film Factory, Oslo
Producer
Lasse Sæther/Roy Anderson
Director
Ingar Amundsen
Lighting Cameraman
Stein Holmberg
Music
**Jacques Offenbach/
Oistein Boassen**

Determined to prove that some goods at Rema 1000 must be expensive Mr Bean has invented a price radar that will expose any high prices.
>Before entering the Rema 1000 shop he tests the radar on his own car and a Jaguar.
>In the shop he gets more and more frustrated because the radar is unable to find anything expensive...until suddenly the radar gives the "expensive" signal.
>But the expensive item turns out to be a lady's watch.
>Again the radar gives the "expensive" signal.
Triumphantly Mr Bean follows the signal certain that he has finally found one of the expensive goods that has to be there.
>But again he is wrong, and this time dangerously wrong.
Our prices will stand up to any test. Rema 1000.

Baby
Advertising Agency
Lowe Howard-Spink, London
Client
Tesco Stores
Creative Director
Paul Weinberger
Copywriter
Phil Dearman
Art Director
Charles Inge
Agency Producer
Charles Crisp
Production Company
**Paul Weiland Film Company,
London**
Producer
Paul Rothwell
Director
Frank Budgen
Lighting Cameraman
Adrian Wild
Music
David Motion

Music throughout.
>This film consists of a series
of beautiful and witty portraits
of babies. Each black and white
portrait has a different colour
tint to it.
>Fade to a little baby sitting
in a huge wicker chair looking
at the camera.
"Because you can't talk."
Fade to a baby boy dressed as a
perfect little farmer. He is
strapped in to a baby bouncer
which is being held up by his
dad.
"Because you can't walk."
Fade to five babies climbing
over a sofa.
"Because your mother has only
got one pair of hands."
Fade to two babies sitting on
a sofa.
"Because you're wonderful...
except when you're hungry."
Fade to baby asleep on a sofa.
"Because you woke your mother
six times last night."
Fade to a baby amongst shopping
bags.
"Because you hate shopping."
Fade to a very grumpy looking
baby standing in a small kitchen
bin.
>Fade to a baby in a Tesco's
baby changing room.
"Because of all these things, at
Tesco we're providing you with
your very own fully equipped
changing room..."
Fade to two children sitting in
a trolley.
"Your own custom-made trolley."
>Fade to a beautifully-lit shot
of a baby holding a milk bottle.
"And we'll even warm your milk
for you."
Fade to a baby on a staircase,
waving.

Better buy cat food at MIGROS.

Vacuum cleaners too.

Cat
Advertising Agency
Comsult/
Advico Young & Rubicam, Zürich
Client
Migros Genossenschafts-Bund
Creative Director
Hansjörg Zürcher
Copywriter
Hansjörg Zürcher
Art Director
Mathias Babst
Production Company
Wirz & Fraefel Productions,
Zürich
Producer
Stefan Fraefel/Pierrot Egger
Director
Ernst Wirz
Lighting Cameraman
Roli Schmid
Music
Crazy Tunes

A nice looking lady lovingly prepares a garnished meal for her cat. The lighting and styling are exactly the same as in a classic cat food commercial.
>The cat sniffs the food and is disgusted. Angry, he smashes the plate. The table falls over and there is a mess on the floor.
"Better buy cat food at Migros."
>The lady begins cleaning up the mess with a vacuum cleaner. The cat strolls too close to the vacuum cleaner and is sucked into the machine.
"Vacuum cleaners too."
Migros.

Better learn French at MIGROS.

Italian too.

And obviously English.

Language Problems
Advertising Agency
Comsult/
Advico Young & Rubicam, Zürich
Client
Migros Genossenschafts-Bund
Creative Director
Hansjörg Zürcher
Copywriter
Hansjörg Zürcher
Art Director
Mathias Babst
Production Company
Wirz & Fraefel Productions,
Zürich
Producer
Stefan Fraefel/Pierrot Egger
Director
Ernst Wirz
Lighting Cameraman
Philippe Cordey
Music
Crazy Tunes

French, Italian and English music is played throughout, interrupted by the Migros jingle. >A young male tourist stands at the Place de la Concorde in Paris with a dictionary in his hand. He politely asks a French woman a question. She looks shocked and slaps his face. "Better learn French at Migros." >The same tourist stands in front of the Colosseum in Rome and asks a beautiful Italian girl a question. Her answer too is a slap in the face. "Italian too." When the same tourist asks a question in London's Picadilly Circus, the reaction of the bowler-hatted businessman is a little too friendly. "And obviously English." Migros.

TRY OUR NEW

FRENCH FRIES

PANS & COMPANY

Potatoes
Advertising Agency
Delvico Bates Barcelona
Client
Pans & Company
Creative Director
Toni Segarra/
Félix Fernandez de Castro
Copyriter
Javier Carro
Art Director
David Caballero
Agency Producer
Lluís Puntes
Production Company
Pespuntes, Barcelona
Director
Lluís Puntes
Lighting Cameraman
Lluís Puntes

Humphrey Bogart and a woman are
speaking. They look worried.
"Well, it's true. They have got
something new at Pans & Company."
"What?"
"Try for yourself."
Bogart gives the woman french
fries by Pans & Company.
"That's all we needed, french
fries. What are we going to do."
"Eat them I guess."
Pans & Company.

Television and Cinema
Retail Stores, Chains and
Restaurants
p.240/241

We blow up your favorite holiday picture!

TIME FOTO
1-Hour Photo

Snapshot
Advertising Agency
Leo Burnett, Oslo
Client
Timefoto
Copywriter
Oistein Borge
Art Director
Johan Gulbranson
Agency Producer
Knut E. Jensen
Production Company
Leo Film, Oslo
Producer
Knut E. Jensen
Director
Johan Gulbranson
Lighting Cameraman
Kjell Vassdal
Music
Bohren & Aaserud

On a beach in southern Europe two elderly women are enjoying a moment of sun.
>Along come two younger local men. They stop when they see the two women. Adjacent to the women, on a small side table, lies an unattended camera. The men exchange a glance, then one of them sneaks up and grabs the camera.
>He returns to his friend, hands him the camera and quickly lowers his pants. His friend snaps a close-up of his private parts.
>Smiling mischieviously they return the camera to the table and leave.
>We blow up your favourite holiday picture!
Timefoto. 1 hour photo.

María   Andrea

FOTOPRIX

Lo mejor, en foto

Eurobest Award Winner
Babies
Advertising Agency
**Casadevall Pedreño & PRG,
Barcelona**
Client
Fotoprix
Creative Director
José Maria Pujol
Copywriter
José Maria Pujol
Art Director
Enric Aguilera
Agency Producer
Pepe Rosas/Mònica Costa
Production Company
Errecerre, Barcelona
Producer
Esteve Riera
Director
Xavier Roselló
Lighting Cameraman
Rafa Lluch
Music
Librería

We see two babies, Maria and
Andrea, on a white background,
peacefully asleep.
>Maria, although she was born on
the same day, at the same time
and weighed the same as Andrea,
is 30% bigger.
>Finally a hand appears from the
top of the screen and we realize
that Maria is a photo.
>The voice-over explains that
now Fotoprix will give you
photos 30% larger for the same
price.

Fotoprix.

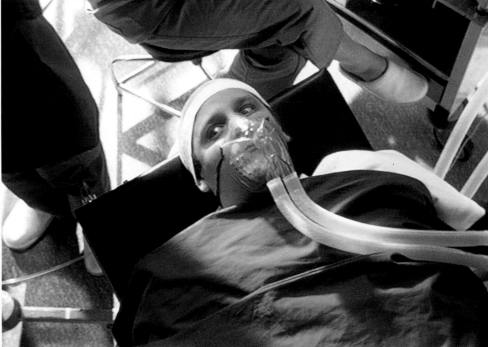

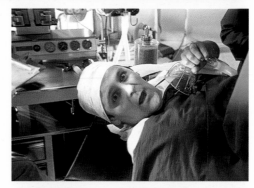

This commercial takes place in an operating theatre.

>During a routine operation, surgeons discover that their patient's illness is going to take longer to treat than they thought.

>Briefly, they speculate on the damage that this is likely to do to his career.

>Just then, the patient appears to wake up. He listens, appalled, as they casually chat about his troubles. After his initial shock however, the man appears to feel better. He lip-syncs to a music soundtrack which suddenly fills the theatre. It's a Nat King Cole recording of 'Let's Face the Music and Dance.'

>At first, the surgeons and nurses are oblivious to his behaviour. Then gradually, all their movements become synchronised with the music.

>As the song ends, the patient happily takes a luxurious gulp from his oxygen mask and goes back to sleep.

>You needn't worry if your life changes. Allied Dunbar Financial Plans adapt, to help you cope with the unexpected.

Allied Dunbar. For the life you don't yet know.

Theatre
Advertising Agency
Grey London
Client
Allied Dunbar
Creative Director
Mike Elliott/Slim Foster
Copywriter
Martin Loraine
Art Director
Steve Jones
Agency Producer
Amanda Lowit
Production Company
Rose Hackney Productions, London
Producer
Ron Holbrook
Director
Graham Rose
Lighting Cameraman
Tony Pierce-Roberts
Music
'Lets Face the Music & Dance':
Irving Berlin/Arr:S.Franglin

Cubicle
Advertising Agency
Grey London
Client
Allied Dunbar
Creative Director
Mike Elliott/Slim Foster
Copywriter
Martin Loraine
Art Director
Steve Jones
Agency Producer
Amanda Lowit
Production Company
Rose Hackney Productions, London
Producer
Ron Holbrook
Director
Graham Rose
Lighting Cameraman
Tony Pierce-Roberts
Music
'Let's Face the Music & Dance':
Irving Berlin/Arr: S Franglin

This commercial takes place in a company washroom.
>Two businessmen are gossiping about the enforced 'retirement' of Morrison, one of their colleagues.
>Unknown to them, Morrison is in one of the toilet cubicles. He's hearing the news for the first time.
>He looks stunned. Then, to the embarrassment of the businessmen, he leaves the cubicle and joins them at the wash-basins.
>After his initial shock, the man appears to feel better. So much so, that he lip-syncs to a music soundtrack which suddenly fills the room. It's a Nat King Cole recording of 'Let's Face the Music and Dance.'
>At first, the other men are oblivious to his behaviour. Then gradually, they too are affected by the music. Their everyday actions become synchronised to the rhythm.
>As the song ends, Morrison walks confidently out of the washroom.
>You needn't worry if your life changes. Allied Dunbar Financial Plans adapt, to help you cope with the unexpected.
Allied Dunbar. For the Life you don't yet know.

A man has just finished having
dinner in an Indian restaurant
and finds that he is short of
cash.
"Don't be angry now but we have
a minor problem."
"It's the money, not the food,
the money!"

The Restaurant
Advertising Agency
Aggerborgs, Stockholm
Client
Sparbankskort
Copywriter
Rolf Lundqvist
Art Director
Richard Hammarskiöld
Production Company
Rally TV, Stockholm
Producer
Henrik Ihre
Director
Johan Rheborg
Lighting Cameraman
Ulf Renneus

"I haven't enough money on me so
I have to go to the hotel to get
money for you so I can pay."
"Can I do that?"
He is met with icy silence from
the restaurant staff.
"I will say you are not very
cooperative. That's not the way
we do business in Sweden.
We say to each other: OK, rita
upp det pa krita, (put it on my
tab) or whatever..."
"Come on here, you can trust me,
I'm Swedish!"
Sparbankskort.
An Easier Way to Pay.

The voice-over announces Tales of the Black Horse — The Swift Deeds.
>We open on a brave knight standing next to a fine medieval tent with a flag on top.
"Once there was a brave knight who lived in temporary accommodation."
The knight is pleased.
"'Tis a very fine tent."
"Until he met a troll."
Cut to an evil troll swinging a huge axe. He knocks the tent down and comes after the knight.
"And now it's a very fine flat."
The knight parries and falls back.
"Now, that troll was one of the most vicious of trolls and utterly remorseless; he pursued that poor knight..."
Cut to a moor. The knight continues to retreat from the stronger troll.
>Cut to an icy waste at night as the troll again advances.
"...over forest and over moor, until by good fortune the knight chanced on a Lloyds Bank."
Cut to the knight still parrying the troll, he walks backwards through an open door into a medieval Lloyds Bank.
"There and then he was offered a Lloyds Bank mortgage."
The exhausted knight holds off the troll as the bank manager explains the mortgage. The knight is overjoyed. In order to sign the deeds they swap places, the manager holding off the troll while the knight signs.
"To help our hero's home become a castle."
Cut to the knight proudly standing on the ramparts of his castle, grinning down at the troll who can't get in.
>Just then two huge shadows loom over the knight. He looks round to see gigantic Mummy and Daddy trolls looking for their offspring.
>They exclaim:
"Oi Quentin, come 'ere."
"Sadly, they could do nothing about the neighbours."
Cut to a Black Horse which stands on a rocky crag in a magical landscape. It rears up majestically.
"The swift mortgage. Another legendary service from Lloyds Bank."

Lloyds Bank.
The Thoroughbred Bank.

Swift Deeds
Advertising Agency
Lowe Howard-Spink, London
Client
Lloyds Bank
Creative Director
Paul Weinberger
Copywriter
Derek Apps
Art Director
Vince Squibb
Agency Producer
Sue Braley
Production Company
Park Village Productions, London
Producer
Mike Stones
Director
Roger Woodburn
Lighting Cameraman
Mike Garfath
Music
**Brahms: Arr. Joe Campbell/
Paul Hart**

Television and Cinema
Banking, Financial and Insurance
p.246/247

Just call us.

Two young men, who are about to take their first flying lesson in a glider, are airborne together. As we see their two instructors together on the ground, we realise that their students have mistaken each other for flying instructors. **Just call us. Centraal Beheer. The Insurance Company.**

Centraal Beheer

**The insurance company
in Apeldoorn. (055·798000)**

Latham is in Hong Kong
overseeing the security for a
high level meeting between the
governor of Hong Kong and the
Chinese Head of State. Due to
the importance of the event,
Latham's boss Sir Brian, is in
the security room with three
Chinese officials. Latham has
only just started to take
control of the proceedings when
he is interrupted by a phone
call from his mother.
"Hello mother...of course I
remembered...Happy Birthday."
He explains to a surprised Sir
Brian that 'Mother' is the code
name for their man in Shanghai.
>Latham realises that he has
forgotten to send flowers and
signals for Bough to make a
quick call. Bough enquires
whether the flowers are to be
daffodils or tulips and what
colour they should be.
>Amid the confusion of different
phones, microphones, security
codes and choice of flowers, a
rather bemused Latham shouts
out:
"Red..." causing a red alert.
Unaware of the ensuing chaos,
Latham smiles at Sir Brian
whilst behind him on the screen
the Chinese Head of State is
being bundled inelegantly down
the stairs and out of the
building.
>Latham bids his mother goodbye.
"Yes, mother, yes I love you
too."
Sir Brian and the officials
stand open-mouthed in amazement.
Latham misunderstands their
stares of disbelief. He explains
that he and 'Mother' were at
Cambridge together.
Barclaycard.

Chinese Take-Away
Advertising Agency
BMP DDB Needham, London
Client
Barclaycard
Creative Director
Tony Cox
Copywriter
Jon Matthews
Art Director
Peter Gatley
Agency Producer
Howard Spivey
Production Company
Tiger Aspect Productions, London
Producer
Glynis Sanders
Director
Mark Chapman
Lighting Cameraman
Tony Pierce-Roberts
Music
Howard Goodall

Television and Cinema
Banking, Financial and Insurance
p.248/249

For full written details of Barclaycard services and conditions, dial 100 Freefone Barclaycard.

Teapot
Advertising Agency
BMP DDB Needham, London
Client
Barclaycard
Creative Director
Tony Cox
Copywriter
Jon Matthews
Art Director
Peter Gatley
Agency Producer
Howard Spivey
Production Company
Tiger Aspect Productions, London
Producer
Glynis Sanders
Director
Mark Chapman
Lighting Cameraman
Tony Pierce-Roberts
Music
Howard Goodall

It is the wedding of the daughter of Sir Brian, the head of the MI7. Latham arrives late with the department's wedding present, a china teapot which he has bought with the company whip-round of seventy-five pounds and fourteen pence.
>Bough asks whether he has used Barclaycard.
>Latham scornfully retorts—
"Oh yes, Bough. I had a manila envelope stuffed with cash and so naturally I used Barclaycard." Bough points out the insurance advantages to Latham's disgust. "Bough! This is the wedding of the daughter of the Head of MI7. There are four men on the roof, two in the choir and the Vicar has no previous convictions. I think that is ample insurance for a china teapot."
After this outburst, Latham rather inappropriately sits on the teapot. We hear the sound of broken china.
Barclaycard.

Nu kan alla teckna fallskärmsavtal

Handelsbanken

Television and Cinema
Banking, Financial and Insurance
p.250/251

Airplane
Advertising Agency
Rönnberg McCann, Stockholm
Client
Handelsbanken
Copywriter
Peter Kandimaa/Bo Rönnberg
Art Director
Mats Alinder
Production Company
Studio 24, Stockholm
Producer
Per Arte
Director
Roy Andersson
Lighting Cameraman
Istvan Borbas

A stewardess shows some
businessmen how to secure their
parachutes.
"...fasten the belts like
this..."
They diligently make the
adjustments. Then the men jump
out of the plane one by one .
>After the last man jumps the
stewardess follows them, bidding
the remaining passengers goodbye
before she jumps.
>The pilots walk through the
cabin and they also jump out of
the plane.
>The passengers look at each
other extremely confused.
**Now everyone can have parachute
insurance. Handelsbanken.**

Lennart

Advertising Agency
Rönnberg McCann, Stockholm

Client
Handelsbanken

Copywriter
Peter Kandimaa/Bo Rönnberg

Art Director
Mats Alinder

Production Company
Studio 24, Stockholm

Producer
Per Arte

Director
Roy Andersson

Lighting Cameraman
Istvan Borbas

The businessmen stand in a pond with parachutes lying around them.
>They call to one another.
>One notices that his tax-free liquor survived.
"My bottles are okay, but where is Lennart?"
"Lennart?"
"He had a parachute, didn't he?"
Now everyone can have parachute insurance. Handelsbanken.

Love Letter
Advertising Agency
Nova Publicidade, Lisbon
Client
CTT Correios de Portugal
Creative Director
Eduardo Martins
Copywriter
Judite Mota
Art Director
Pedro Ferreira
Agency Producer
Eduardo Martins
Production Company
Abacate
Producer
José Torres
Director
Carlos Lopes
Lighting Cameraman
Carlos Lopes

A very fat woman sits on a couch
reading a letter. As she reads
on, she seems more and more
surprised:
"My love, your beautiful blue
eyes keep coming to my mind. I
dream of your red cherry lips,
your sculptural body, your long,
golden hair. You are beautiful.
I wish to hold you in my arms to
worship and admire your ethereal
beauty."
**Watch out! The Postal Codes have
changed. Make sure you have the
new codes. Codigo Postal.**

Sleeper
Advertising Agency
Forsman & Bodenfors, Gothenburg
Client
Posten
Copywriter
Björn Engström
Art Director
Staffan Forsman/Mark Whitehouse
Production Company
Adaptor Moland, Copenhagen
Producer
Bévort/Ejlers
Director
Kristian Levring
Lighting Cameraman
Karl Oskarsson

We hear traffic noises and bed-springs creaking.
>A man is twisting and turning in a hotel bed, trying to get to sleep. Street noise and a neon light flashing through his window are keeping him awake. He turns on the light, reaches for the post catalogue on his bedside table, and starts reading.
"Postage costs..registered letters...foreign currency... parcel post...home giro... private pension schemes... changing address..." Yawning, he finally falls asleep.
**The new Post Catalogue.
Boring but useful.**

Eurobest Campaign Award Winner
A Telephone Call Prolongs Life
Spaghetti Carbonara
Advertising Agency
Armando Testa, Milan
Client
Telecom Italia
Creative Director
Mauro Mortaroli
Copywriter
Erminio Perocco/Mauro Mortaroli
Art Director
Manuele Mariani/
Alessandro Brunetti
Production Company
Film Master
Director
Alessandro D'Alatri
Lighting Cameraman
Giuseppe Lanci
Editor
Roberto Crescenzi
Client Director
Enzo Giacopinelli/
Marco Piazzoli
Music
Gabriele Ducros

A Foriegn Legion firing squad
prepare to execute their victim.
The man is asked if he has a
last wish and he asks to make a
telephone call. He telephones
his friend Mario and they
discuss getting together on
Sunday. Our man says the journey
takes too long. He prefers to
talk on the phone.
>They continue to chat and he is
about to ring off, until he
hears that Marco is also there.
He asks to speak to him. The
conversation continues. The
firing squad continue to wait...

The conversation continues while
the firing squad wait in the
sweltering sun. The conversation
moves on to the recipe for
spaghetti carbonara and whether
or not to add garlic. Our man
asks the opinion of the firing
squad.

Eurobest Campaign Award Winner
Everaldo
Without Telephone
You Call I Call
Advertising Agency
Armando Testa, Milan
Client
Telecom Italia
Creative Director
Mauro Mortaroli
Copywriter
Erminio Perocco/Mauro Mortaroli
Art Director
Manuele Mariani/
Alessandro Brunetti
Production Company
Film Master
Director
Alessandro D'Alatri
Lighting Cameraman
Giuseppe Lanci
Editor
Roberto Crescenzi
Client Director
Enzo Giacopinelli/
Marco Piazzoli
Music
Gabriele Ducros

As night falls, the firing squad prepares to go to sleep but our man is still on the telephone. He is talking baby-talk to Marco's new son Everaldo. The General also listens in and says he sounds cute...

It is the next day. The firing squad are preparing for the execution again. Our man is still on the telephone and says, "Without the telephone, I would be dead."

Finally the firing squad are leaving the fort, leaving only one guard. Our man is still talking on the telephone and stops only to ask them to close the door behind them.

Foreigners.
Without them our economy
will stand still.

Racist
Advertising Agency
Advico Young & Rubicam, Zürich
Client
Cash TV
Creative Director
Hansjörg Zürcher
Copywriter
Matthias Freuler
Production Company
**Wirz & Fraefel Productions,
Zürich**
Producer
Stefan Fraefel
Director
Ernst Wirz
Lighting Cameraman
Pierrot Egger

Television and Cinema
Non-Commercial Services and
Political Advertising
p.258/259

A Swiss skinhead bitches about
foreigners in a film report. The
film team — three foreigners —
cut the sound, then the light,
and finally the camera.
**Without foreigners, our economy
will stand still.**

 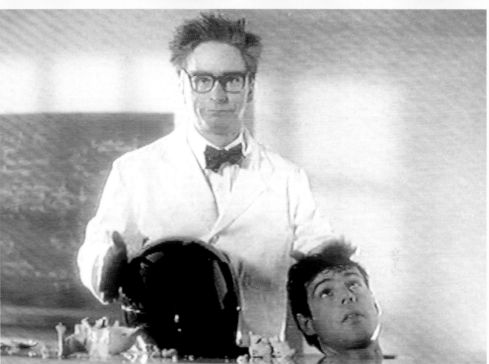

Eurobest Award Winner
Skull
Advertising Agency
EPG.TBWA, Lisbon
Client
Prevenção Rodoviaria Portuguesa
Creative Director
Pedro Bidarra
Copywriter
Pedro Bidarra
Art Director
José Heitor
Agency Producer
Frederico Cerejeiro
Production Company
Shots
Producer
João Egreja

The setting is a laboratory, where a mad scientist in a white coat stands at a counter.
>Resting there side by side is a human skull and a black motorcycle helmet.
"This is a skull like the skull of any biker. And this is a helmet like the helmet of any biker."
He then reaches beneath the counter and picks up a giant sledge-hammer.
"And this is an accident like any other accident."
He swings the hammer and pulverizes the skull in one stroke. Then he also pounds the helmet but it barely moves.
>Now the scientist lifts the helmet to reveal the head of a woozy but otherwise unscathed man poking through a hole in the counter.
>Patting the subject on the head he says:
"As you see you'd better drive by the book."

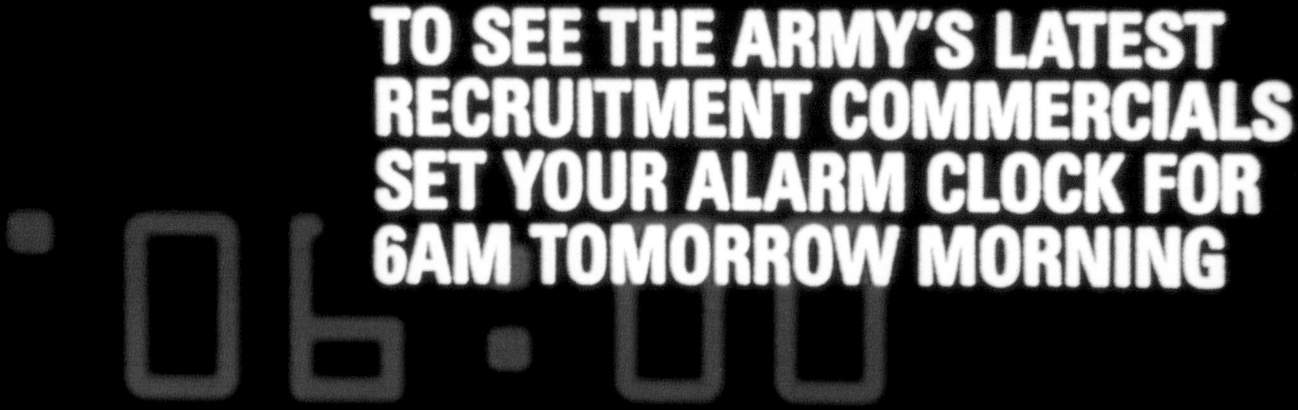

TO SEE THE ARMY'S LATEST RECRUITMENT COMMERCIALS SET YOUR ALARM CLOCK FOR 6AM TOMORROW MORNING

'06:00

Eurobest Award Winner
Launch
Advertising Agency
Saatchi & Saatchi, London
Client
CCO/Army
Creative Director
James Lowther/Simon Dicketts
Copywriter
Adam Kean
Art Director
Alexandra Taylor
Agency Producer
David Eddon
Production Company
Arden Sutherland-Dodd, London
Producer
David Ker
Director
Thomas Krygier
Lighting Cameraman
Giuseppe Maccari

IF YOU THINK YOU KNOW THE ANSWER CALL ARMY OFFICER ON 0345 300 111

OR JOIN THE TERRITORIAL ARMY AT WEEKENDS

DO YOU WANT TO LEARN TO DRIVE?

If you feel ashamed about showing your two breasts

imagine showing just one.

Visit your gynaecologist once a year.

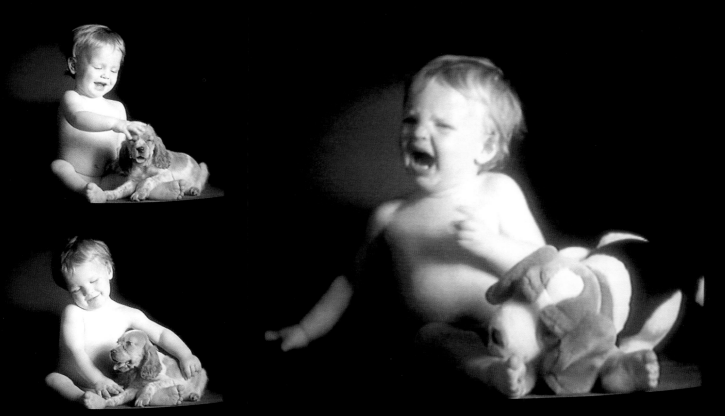

Child & Puppy
Advertising Agency
**Casadevall Pedreño & PRG,
Barcelona**
Client
Adena WWF España
Creative Director
Luis Casadevall
Copywriter
Ángel Sánchez
Art Director
Pepe Rosas
Agency Producer
Pepe Rosas/Mónica Costa
Production Company
Errecerre, Barcelona
Producer
Esteve Riera
Director
Xavier Roselló
Lighting Cameraman
Rafael Lluch
Music
Classic & New

A baby sitting on the floor is
happily playing with a puppy.
The puppy sits beside the baby
and the two of them are having
a wonderful time together.
>Suddenly a hand appears and
replaces the puppy with a fluffy
toy dog. This exchange of a real
puppy for an artificial one
causes the baby to cry
inconsolably.
**Nothing can replace life.
The World Wildlife Fund.**

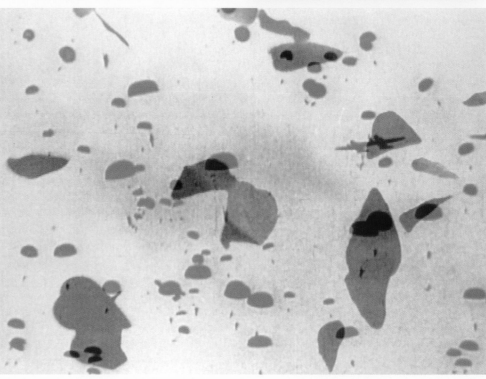

Silence

Advertising Agency
DFSD Bozell, London
Client
The Royal British Legion
Creative Director
Greg Delaney/Brian Stewart
Copywriter
Mark Tweddell
Art Director
Marcus Vinton
Agency Producer
James Tomkinson
Production Company
Produktion, London
Producer
Lewis More O'Ferrell
Director
Brian Griffin
Lighting Cameraman
Steve Tickner

We open on a super which reads:
There now follows a silence in
remembrance of those who
fought for our country.
>We see a poppy wreath, the
camera closes in on the wreath
and goes through the hole.
>We then see a mixture of war
footage from World War II
through to the Gulf, as well as
more contemporary footage
illustrating how the British
Legion helps thousands of ex-
servicemen and their dependants
every year. We will be taken
through the whole gamut of
emotions from despair and
frustration to triumph and joy.
>Another super appears. It
reads: Now please make a noise
for those who still need help.
>We see and hear a collecting
tin being shaken and money
falling into the tin.
**Remember the dead, but don't
forget the living.**

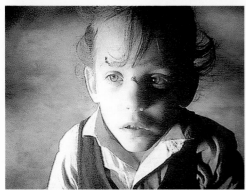

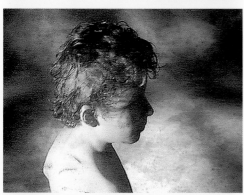

FOUNDATION "OUR HOME"

CHILD PROTECTION

Child Abuse
Advertising Agency
Tandem DDB Needham, Madrid
Client
Fundacion A.N.A.R.
Creative Director
Angel Del Tio
Copywriter
Mauricio Dedalo
Art Director
Jose Luis Pareja
Agency Producer
Yolanda Galant
Production Company
Marcha Films, Madrid
Producer
Gil Carretero
Director
Pascuale Caprile
Lighting Cameraman
Pascuale Caprile

Open on camera. A little boy
with an ill-treated look.
"He's not harassed in Brazil."
Cut to a thirteen year old boy
with the same look.
"He doesn't live in Sarajevo."
Cut to a little girl with the
same look.
"She's not trying to survive in
Calcutta."
Cut to a fifteen year old girl
with the same look.
"She's not fighting in El
Salvador."
Cut to a little boy with the
same look.
"It's all happening in our
country. Their particular hell
is their home. Their enemies are
their own parents."
Cut to a fifteen year old girl
with the same look.
"Help them escape."
Foundation. "Our home."
Child protection.

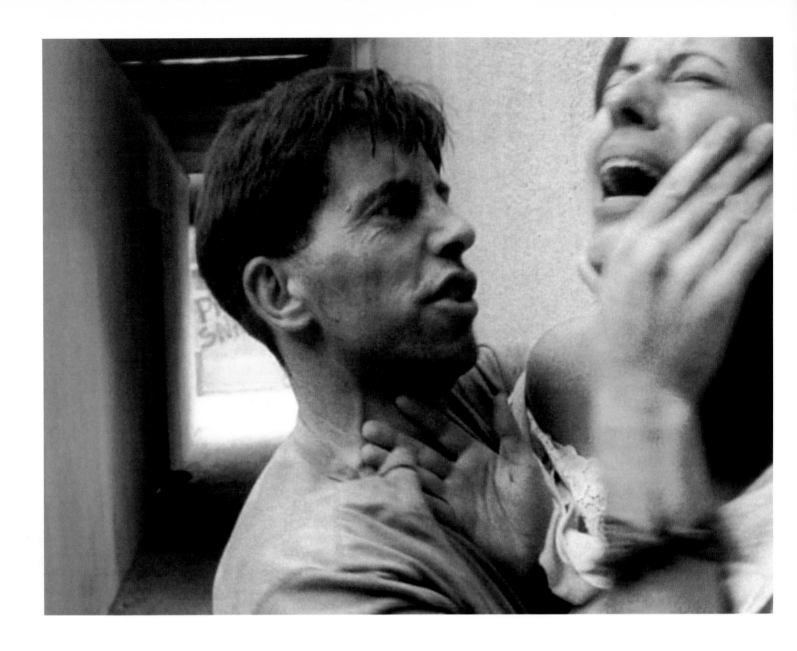

Bosnia
Advertising Agency
New Deal DDB Needham, Oslo
Client
Norwegian Red Cross
Copywriter
Knut Georg Andresen
Art Director
Tone Garmann
Production Company
Big Deal, Oslo
Producer
Turid Øversveen
Director
Morten Tyldum

We hear a car exploding. We witness a violent scene which is taking place down a narrow passage. A group of soldiers are attempting to put a sack over the head of a prisoner who is on his knees. He has been beaten and has apparently given up all hope. His wife, who is being held back by soldiers, is begging for his life. She becomes more and more desperate but the soldiers carry on with the execution.
>The commercial cuts to black and we hear a shot being fired.
Telethon 1993.
Benefit for Victims of War.
Sunday November 14.

Cafe
Advertising Agency
New Deal DDB Needham, Oslo
Client
Norwegian Red Cross
Copywriter
Knut Georg Andresen
Art Director
Tone Garmann
Production Company
Big Deal, Oslo
Producer
Turid Øversveen
Director
Morten Tyldum

Scenes of horror and war are intercut with scenes of calm and tranquillity in a downtown cafe. The scenes from the cafe have an aggressive soundtrack suggestive of guns and bombs, whilst the scenes from the warzone have a carefree cheerful soundtrack.

Telethon 1993.
Benefit for Victims of War.
Sunday November 14.

Eurobest Award Winner
Alone
Advertising Agency
New Deal DDB Needham, Oslo
Client
Norwegian Red Cross
Copywriter
Knut Georg Andresen
Art Director
Tone Garmann
Production Company
Big Deal, Oslo
Producer
Turid Øversveen
Director
Mona Hoel

An old lady wakes up in her bedroom. For a brief moment she imagines her husband is standing by her bed but when she is fully awake she realises that it is a dream.

>She gets up, dresses and goes downstairs. She does some dusting, listens to the radio and daydreams her way through the afternoon. Later she falls asleep in front of the TV. She goes back upstairs and gets ready for bed.

"Do you know someone who is alone this Easter? Call them."
Norwegian Red Cross.

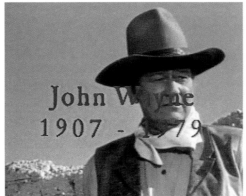

Famous
Advertising Agency
Delvico Bates Barcelona
Client
**Spanish Cancer Association
(AECC)**
Creative Director
**Toni Segarra/
Félix Fernandez de Castro**
Copywriter
Javier Carro
Art Director
David Caballero
Agency Producer
Lluís Puntes
Production Company
**Ricardo Albiñana Films,
Barcelona**
Producer
Ricard Albiñana Jr.
Director
Ricard Albiñana Jr.

Pictures showing the birth and
death dates of some famous
people.
>Another ad using famous people
to get hold of your money.
**The Spanish Cancer Association.
A million thanks.**

Helfen Sie helfen

Only One Plus
Advertising Agency
Unique, Vienna
Client
The Red Cross of Vienna
Creative Director
Mark Nevosad
Copywriter
Christian Strasser
Art Director
Heinz Nevosad
Production Company
Filmhaus Wien
Producer
Thomas Brunner
Director
Lila Schwarzenberg
Lighting Cameraman
Archiv
Music
Tic-Music

We see a red bar which depicts
scenes of violence and suffering.
"In a world of minus there's one
plus."
"Help us help."
The Red Cross Vienna.

The Recorder
Advertising Agency
Stenström & Co., Stockholm
Client
Trygg Hansa/
Svenska Livräddn Sällskapet
Copywriter
Karin Bille
Art Director
Hans Ahlgren
Production Company
Anima Film, Stockholm
Producer
Robert Reiss-Andersen
Director
Erik Gustafsson

Two parallel stories are being told:
>In a room a young girl is playing a typical Swedish summer tune on her recorder.
>By a river a young boy is balancing on a log.
>The girl continues to play. The boy's older brother is waiting on the shore.
>The young boy suddenly loses his balance and falls into the water.
>The girl continues to play.
>The older brother runs towards the water; the boy is gasping for air.
>The older brother rescues him.
>The girl continues to play.
>She inhales for the finale.
>The boy inhales in order to give mouth to mouth resuscitation to his brother.
>The girl finishes her playing.
Learn how to play an important part in someone's life as well.

Big & Orange
Advertising Agency
Lowe Howard-Spink, London
Client
Coca-Cola
Creative Director
Paul Weinberger
Copywriter
John Silver
Art Director
Kevin Thomas
Agency Producer
Mike Hazledine
Production Company
Bolex Brothers, Bristol
Producer
Richard Hutchinson
Director
Dave Borthwick
Lighting Cameraman
Andy MacCormack
Music
Chris Blackwell

In a bizarre futuristic
landscape, we see a Fanta tanker
standing at a derelict
truckstop.
>An elephant made out of metal
parts (Elefanta) approaches,
scaring off other small metallic
creatures.
>Unscrewing the cap on the
tanker with his trunk, he drinks
the tanker dry. The orange
liquid courses through his
tubes, the washing machine in
his tummy fills up, his body
expands.
>The tanker buckles and crumples.
>Loud guitar music strikes up
as, invigorated, he strolls off
down the road, giving a
triumphant kick with his hind
legs.
>As he does this, his body turns
orange.
Fanta

Unchain Your Brain

Advertising Agency
BMP DDB Needham, London
Client
Beauty International
Creative Director
Tony Cox
Copywriter
Alasdair Graham
Art Director
Frazer Jelleyman
Agency Producer
Michael Parker
Production Company
Partizan, London
Producer
Toby Courlander/George Berman
Director
Michel Gondry
Lighting Cameraman
Eric Valin
Music
Water Music

Men in sci-fi vehicles are working laboriously in a vast subterranean factory.
>The instant the hooter sounds, they stop work and file out.
>An overhead device plucks the men from the vehicles, leaving them free to move and stretch their bodies. Their bodies grow to normal size and proportions.
>Once out of the factory and into the daylight, the men throw themselves into playing a sci-fi sport.
>Tiny projectiles are fired into the air, which expand to become huge, brightly-coloured, gravity-defying spheres.
>We pull back, at fast speed, to the bottle of Adidas fragrance:
Adidas Aftershave.
Unchain Your Brain.

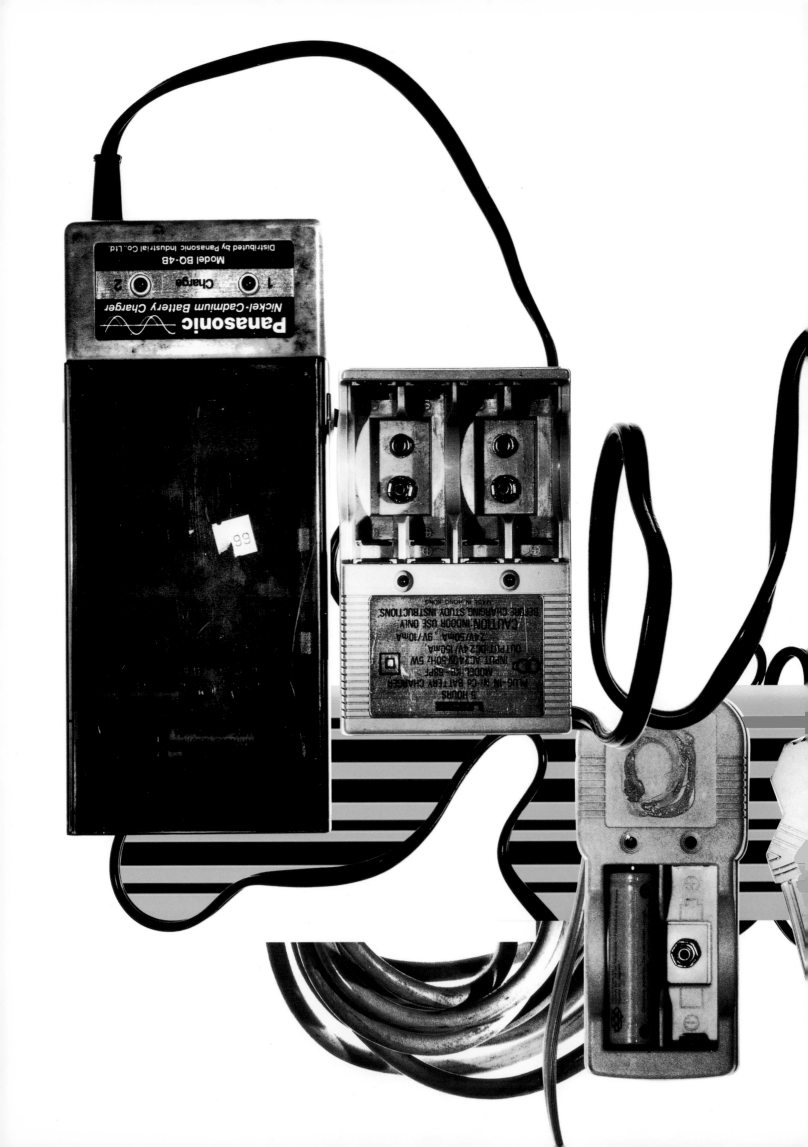

Rubicam Italia
Anders Weinar, Creative Director, TBWA Italia
Cesare Casiraghi, Creative Director, Bates Italia
Valeria Monti, Managing Director, Lintas Milano
Alberto Contri, Managing Director, Medicus Intercon
Pio Dolci, KJS
Milka Pogliani, Creative Director, McCann-Erickson Italiana
Alberto De Martini, Creative Director, Ata Tonic Milan

The Netherlands
Béla Stamenkovits, Art Director, Campaign Company
Matthijs van Wensveen, Creative Director, FHV/BBDO
Pieter van Velzen, Creative Director, Lowe Kuiper & Schouten
Harold Hamersma, Creative Director, Publicis.FCB/Prad
André van Leeuwen, Art Director, DMB&B Advertising
Peter van Wijk, Creative Director, Bruns van der Wijk
Bob More, Copywriter, Wieden & Kennedy
Peter Zeehandelaar, Copywriter, Hunky Dory
Rob Sluijs, Creative Director, KKBR
Martin Cornelissen, Art Director, PMSvW/Y&R

Norway
Johan Gulbranson, Creative, Leo Burnett
Eivind Solberg, Art Director, JBR Reklambyrå
Else Haavik, Art Director, FCB
Morten Foss, Art Director, New Deal DDB Needham
Morten Varhaug, Art Director, Bates Backer Spielvogel
Owen Willis, Creative Director, La Familia
Ragnar Roksvåg, Copywriter, Bold
Morten Thoresen, Copywriter, Ogilvy & Mather
Kenneth Hansen, Creative Director, Binders
Leif Brekke, Creative Director, Myers Lintas

Spain
Jordi Vilajoana Rovira, President, Tiempo/BBDO
David Caballero, Creative Director, Delvico Bates Barcelona
Ana Hidalgo, Creative Director, Contrapunto
Juan Campmany, Managing Director, Tandem DDB Needham Campmany Guasch
José Guerrero, President, TBWA
Marcelo Delgado, Creative Director, Lintas Madrid
José Luis Esteo, Creative Director, Alta Definición
José Gamo Suarez, Creative

Director, RZR/Scali McCabe Sloves

Sweden
Christer Alm, Copy Director, Alm & Co.
Carl Lewenhaupt, Copywriter, Rönnberg McCann
Axel Laubscher, Director, Mekano Film & Television
Mark Whitehouse, Art Director, Forsman & Bodenfors
Petter Ödeen, Art Director, Garbergs Annonsbyra
Rosita Johnsson, Art Director, Allansson & Nilsson
Linus Karlsson, Creative Director, Paradiset DDB Needham
Stefan Rönnquist, Copywriter, Alinder & Co.

Switzerland
Richard Schweizer, Creative Director, Lintas Zürich
Martin Spillman, Creative Director, Advico Young & Rubicam
Martin Denecke, Manager/Chairman, GGK Basel
Edi Andrist, Creative Director, Andrist
Francis Sulzer, Creative Director, Sulzer & Sutter
Daniel Matter, Managing Director, Matter Leo Burnett
Frank Bodin, Creative Director, Aebi Strebel
Remy Fabrikant, Creative Director, Schmid & Hostettler

& Fabrikant
Hanspeter Schweizer, Creative Director, Wirz Werbeagentur

Packaging/Design Jury
Rob van den Berg, Managing Director, Milford van den Berg Design, Netherlands
Romano Scuvée, Managing Director, Motive Global Design Consultants, Belgium
Soren Salling-Petersen, Managing Director, Inter Profil, Denmark
Jean Michel Farce, Director, I G Design, France
Nick Meyer, Partner, Brösske Meyer & Ruf, Germany
John Larkin, Managing Director Design House Consultants, Great Britain
Philippe Guignard, Partner, Ard Graphic, Switzerland
Maria Gemma Del Corno, Art Director, Design Group Italia, Italy
Teun Anders, Owner, Visser Bay Anders Toscani, Netherlands
Rosemary Blandy, Manager, Pineapple Design, Portugal
Victor Mirabet, Director, Schmidlin & Partners Barcelona, Spain

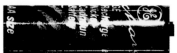

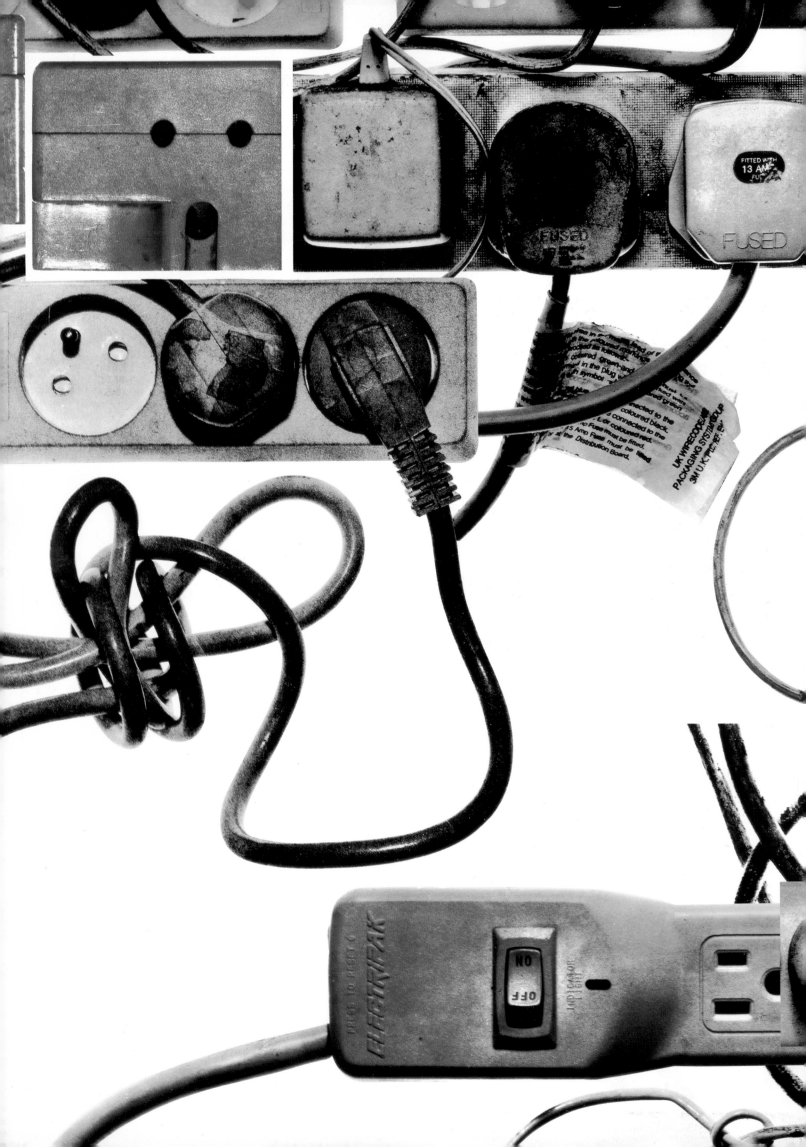